THE WAY
PEOPLE
LIVE

Life During the Spanish Inquisition

Titles in The Way People Live series include:

THE WAY
PEOPLE
LIVE

Life During the Spanish Inquisition

by Gail B. Stewart

Lucent Books, P.O. Box 289011, San Diego, CA 92198-9011

Library of Congress Cataloging-in-Publication Data

Stewart, Gail, 1949–
    Life during the Spanish Inquisition / by Gail B. Stewart.
        p.   cm. — (The way people live)
    Includes bibliographical references and index.
    Summary: Examines the culture of Spain during the centuries of the
Inquisition by focusing on personal aspects of daily life at the time.
    ISBN 1-56006-346-7
    1. Inquisition—Spain—Juvenile literature.   2. Spain—Church history—
Juvenile literature.   [1. Inquisition.   2. Spain—Church history.]   I. Title.
II. Series.
    BX1735.S74   1998
    272'.2—dc21   97–17709
                                                                                   CIP
                                                                                   AC

Printed in the U.S.A.

Contents

Discovering the Humanity in Us All

The Way People Live series focuses on pockets of human culture. Some of these are current cultures, like the Eskimos of the Arctic; others no longer exist, such as the Jewish ghetto in Warsaw during World War II. What many of these cultural pockets share, however, is the fact that they have been viewed before, but not completely understood.

To really understand any culture, it is necessary to strip the mind of the common notions we hold about groups of people. These stereotypes are the archenemies of learning. It does not even matter whether the stereotypes are positive or negative; they are confining and tight. Removing them is a challenge that's not easily met, as anyone who has ever tried it will admit. Ideas that do not fit into the templates we create are unwelcome visitors—ones we would prefer remain quietly in a corner or forgotten room.

The cowboy of the Old West is a good example of such confining roles. The cowboy was courageous, yet soft-spoken. His time (it is always a he, in our template) was spent alternatively saving a rancher's daughter from certain death on a runaway stagecoach, or shooting it out with rustlers. At times, of course, he was likely to get a little crazy in town after a trail drive, but for the most part, he was the epitome of inner strength. It is disconcerting to find out that the cowboy is human, even a bit childish. Can it really be true that cowboys would line up to help the cook on the trail drive grind coffee, just hoping he would give them a little stick of pep-

permint candy that came with the coffee shipment? The idea of tough cowboys vying with one another to help "Coosie" (as they called their cooks) for a bit of candy seems silly and out of place.

So is the vision of Eskimos playing video games and watching MTV, living in prefab housing in the Arctic. It just does not fit with what "Eskimo" means. We are far more comfortable with snow igloos and whale blubber, harpoons and kayaks.

Although the cultures dealt with in Lucent's The Way People Live series are often historically and socially well known, the emphasis is on the personal aspects of life. Groups of people, while unquestionably affected by their politics and their governmental structures, are more than those institutions. How do people in a particular time and place educate their children? What do they eat? And how do they build their houses? What kinds of work do they do? What kinds of games do they enjoy? The answers to these questions bring these cultures to life. People's lives are revealed in the particulars and only by knowing the particulars can we understand these cultures' will to survive and their moments of weakness and greatness.

This is not to say that understanding politics does not help to understand a culture. There is no question that the Warsaw ghetto, for example, was a culture that was brought about by the politics and social ideas of Adolf Hitler and the Third Reich. But the Jews who were crowded together in the ghetto cannot be understood by the Reich's politics. Their life was a day-to-day battle for existence, and the creativity and methods they used to prolong their lives is a vital story of human perseverance that would be denied by focusing only on the institutions of Hitler's Germany. Knowing that children as young as five or six outwitted Nazi guards on a daily basis, that Jewish policemen helped the Germans control the ghetto, that children attended secret schools in the ghetto and even earned diplomas—these are the things that reveal the fabric of life, that can inspire, intrigue, and amaze.

Books in the The Way People Live series allow both the casual reader and the student to see humans as victims, heroes, and onlookers. And although humans act in ways that can fill us with feelings of sorrow and revulsion, it is important to remember that "hero," "predator," and "victim" are dangerous terms. Heaping undue pity or praise on people reduces them to objects, and strips them of their humanity.

Seeing the Jews of Warsaw only as victims is to deny their humanity. Seeing them only as they appear in surviving photos, staring at the camera with infinite sadness, is limiting, both to them and to those who want to understand them. To an object of pity, the only appropriate response becomes "Those poor creatures!" and that reduces both the quality of their struggle and the depth of their despair. No one is served by such two-dimensional views of people and their cultures.

With this in mind, the The Way People Live series strives to flesh out the traditional, two-dimensional views of people in various cultures and historical circumstances. Using a wide variety of primary quotations—the words not only of the politicians and government leaders, but of the real people whose lives are being examined—each book in the series attempts to show an honest and complete picture of a culture removed from our own by time or space.

By examining cultures in this way, the reader will notice not only the glaring differences from his or her own culture, but also will be struck by the similarities. For indeed, people share common needs—warmth, good company, stability, and affirmation from others. Ultimately, seeing how people really live, or have lived can only enrich our understanding of ourselves.

The Flames and the Heat

The lettering on the yellowed old document is beautiful in the way of handwriting produced in centuries when people took pride in their script. Fancy flourishes on the capital letters give the pages an elegant look, as though it might be a powerful sermon, or a passionate love letter, perhaps. When the Spanish text is translated, however, the beauty of the document fades, and its meaning is horrifying, almost ghoulish.

It is a detailed record of the defendants tried between 1480 and 1490 in the special courts of state and church leaders called the Spanish Inquisition. The document lists the crimes of which those people had been accused and provides a gruesome description of the tortures imposed on those judged to be guilty. The author of the document is Hernando del Pulgar, the secretary of Queen Isabella of Spain.

Banned Books, Witchcraft, and Jewish Holidays

Some of those arrested, the secretary reports, were "new Christians," Jews who had converted

Dungeons of the Inquisition

One of the most notorious prisons of the Spanish Inquisition was located in what is now an opera house in Lisbon. The following account, from Cecil Roth's book The Spanish Inquisition, *is a portion of the description of the prison when it was opened to the pubic for viewing in 1821.*

"Human skull and other bones were found in the dungeons. On the walls of these frightful holes are carved the names of some of the unfortunate victims buried in them, accompanied with lines or notches, indicating the number of days of their captivity. One name had beside it the date of 1809. The doors of certain dungeons, which had not been used for some years, still remained shut, but the people [eventually] forced them open. In nearly all of them, human bones were found, and among these melancholy remains, were, in one dungeon, fragments of the garments of a monk, and his girdle [belt]. In some of these dungeons, the chimney-shaped airhole was walled up, which is a certain sign of the murder of the prisoner. In such cases, the unfortunate victim was compelled to go into the airhole, the lower extremity of which was immediately closed by masonry. Quicklime was afterwards thrown down on him, which extinguished life and destroyed the body."

A session of the Inquisition court. The Inquisition sought to purge Spain of anyone who questioned or contradicted the Catholic Church.

to Christianity under intense pressure from the Inquisition. Many of these new Christians had been discovered keeping Jewish traditions or celebrating Jewish holidays. Others arrested were Catholics who had read books banned by the Inquisition, such as essays by Martin Luther and other Christian theologians who questioned certain practices of the church. Others brought before the court were accused of practicing witchcraft or sorcery. Still other defendants had been overheard criticizing the methods of the court—a dangerous act in Spain in the late fifteenth century.

Pulgar wrote that in the ten years during which he was secretary to the queen, the court sentenced thousands of people to be burned at the stake. Many thousands more were imprisoned, subjected to excruciating forms of torture, or made to endure public humiliation. Hundreds of dead people were tried, as well: their remains were dug out of cemeteries and burned as their children and grandchildren looked on in horror.

Almost everyone charged with a crime was found guilty by the courts of the Spanish Inquisition, whose jurisdiction extended throughout the districts of Spain. Toledo, one of the largest districts, averaged fewer than two acquittals per year. And the few who were formally cleared were viewed with suspicion for the rest of their lives. Says one historian, "In most cases, the formula of acquittal intimated [hinted], not that the accused was innocent, but [only] that the accuser had not been able to prove his case."[1]

The Holy Office

Why were the courts of the Inquisition able to wield such destructive power? The answer is that they were empowered by the Spanish government, with the full cooperation of the Catholic Church. The Inquisition's mission was a broad one: find, try, and punish anyone who was doing anything the inquisitional courts interpreted as being a threat to the power of the Catholic Church in Spain.

Officially, the leaders of the Spanish Inquisition, often referred to as "the Holy Office," were interested in helping wrong-doers realize their mistakes and correct them. In actuality, the emphasis was more on punishing and showing vengeance to the accused than on instructing and forgiving them. As a result, even good Catholics were nervous and afraid. No one wanted to be caught in acts that might look suspicious or anti-Catholic. People were right to worry: the Holy Office could make arrests based on complaints from anyone—neighbors, friends, even one's own children! It was common during the Spanish Inquisition for innocent people to be arrested and punished, just on the word of some enemy, whose identity might never be given in court.

"The Story Is Terrible Enough Without Reducing It to Figures"

Many historians have studied documents that have survived the centuries, trying to get an accurate count of those murdered and other-

Citizens gather to watch a public execution in Seville. During the Inquisition, people lived in fear of falling under the court's deadly scrutiny.

wise victimized by the Inquisition. But Henry Charles Lea, acknowledged to be one of the world's foremost scholars of the Inquisition, thinks such speculation takes away from the true horror of the time. In his *History of the Inquisition in Spain*, Lea urges that it is not as important

> to determine how many human beings the Inquisition consigned to the stake, how many bones it exhumed, how many effigies it burnt, how many penitents [people who confessed to crimes, often after being tortured] it threw into prison or sent to the galleys, how many orphans its confiscation [practice of taking a convicted person's money and property] cast penniless on the world. The story is terrible enough without reducing it to figures. Its awful significance lies in the fact that men were found who consciously did this . . . in the name of the gospel of peace and of Him [Jesus] who came to teach the brotherhood of man.[2]

How did people deal with the stress of living during the time of the Spanish Inquisition? As one expert writes, "Every person who dared to think for himself in matters of faith must have lain down to rest at night shivering with fear, [when] every thinker was a haunted man."[3]

It is difficult to know what it must have been like to live when public executions—burnings at the stake and beheadings—were staged spectacles, as widely attended as sporting events today, when the screams of people being tortured drowned out the sound of church bells, and when one never knew who would be taken next by the Holy Office. For although not everyone in Spain during the Inquisition was doomed to be burned at the stake, almost no one escaped feeling the enormous heat of the fires.

The Making of an Institution

The Inquisition started in France in the early thirteenth century, and by the late Middle Ages it had spread to Germany and Italy. It was not until the late fifteenth century that the Inquisition was eagerly embraced by Spain, where it took an especially vicious form.

The Inquisition began as an arm of the Catholic Church in Europe. Its stated purpose was to preserve the church's power by singling out its enemies—people called heretics, whose actions, or even beliefs, were somehow contrary to the church's teachings. The church hoped that officials of the Inquisition, the "inquisitors," could persuade such people to see the error of their ways and repent. Inevitably, some would refuse this opportunity to renounce their heresies, or forbidden views and practices. It was the purpose of the Inquisition to identify these enemies of the church and remove them from society.

The Church in Medieval Europe

There was a single branch of Christianity in Europe, and that was the Catholic, or universal, Church. Except for the relatively small Jewish communities throughout Europe, and the Moors, an Islamic people from North Africa who had settled in Spain, everyone in medieval Europe was born a Christian.

Every village had a church at its center. It was always the largest building, and its stone construction made it far stronger in times of bad weather or enemy attack than the crude wood and earth huts of the villagers. In addition to housing religious activities, village churches often served as schools or even hospitals. Guild meetings and village council sessions frequently were held in churches.

Although the church affected everyday life and governed many of people's social and cultural activities, medieval Europeans were not particularly pious. In fact, average citizens in that age knew very little about their faith. Priests were usually the only villagers who could read and write, so all that most townspeople knew of Christianity was what they were able to understand from Sunday sermons. (Most of the service was in Latin, but preaching generally was done in the language of the local congregations.)

In most rural areas, people tended to be superstitious, often following a sort of hodgepodge religion—a combination of Christianity and the ancient pagan religions once so powerful in those places. As one historian explains,

> Medieval man could simply not bear to part with [pagan deities such as] Thor, Hermes, Zeus, Juno, Cronus, Saturn, and their peers. Idol worship addressed needs the Church could not meet. Its rituals, myths, legends, marvels, and miracles were particularly suited to people who, living in the trackless fen and impenetrable forest, were always vulnerable to random disaster.[4]

The common people of medieval Europe understood little of the Christianity they were preached and often incorporated their older pagan beliefs into the religion.

Thus many peasants attended mass, yet in their hearts also held the ancient beliefs that far predated the church—and saw nothing wrong with accepting parts of both traditions. Most village priests knew about this division of loyalties and tended to ignore it, rather than attempt the nearly impossible task of forcing them to abandon the old ways.

More Powerful than Kings and Queens

All the village churches, the beautiful cathedrals, and the busy monasteries were controlled by the leader of the church, the pope. He ruled from Rome, and during the Middle Ages his power and authority were enormous. Not only was his the last word on matters of the clergy, church policy, and religious dogma and belief, but papal authority seeped into the world of politics and matters of state.

Kings and queens began to look to Rome for the pope's advice on their actions.

A Key Role in Politics

One reason for the church's broad authority was the perceived wisdom of the pope. By the church's definition, the office of the Holy Father, as he was often called, was closer to God than to humanity. Another reason was the growing belief that the very power of kings and queens came from God and had to be officially conferred by the church. This belief in the so-called divine rights of kings was virtually unchallenged during the Middle Ages.

The practice began during medieval times of having a high church official—a cardinal or archbishop—attend the coronation of a king or queen and actually place the crown on his or her head. The placing of the crown was followed by a ceremony in which the new ruler

No Sense of Self

An aspect of medieval life that modern observers find especially difficult to grasp is the complete lack of ego, or sense of self, that characterized men and women in those days. In an age that rarely required a last name, and in which people almost never traveled, few had the ability or the perspective to see themselves in a larger picture, as William Manchester explains in A World Lit Only by Fire: The Medieval Mind and the Renaissance.

"Even those with creative powers had no sense of self. Each of the great soaring medieval cathedrals, our most treasured legacy from that age, required three or four centuries to complete. . . . [We] know nothing of the architects or builders. They were glorifying God. To them their identity in this life was irrelevant. Nobles had surnames, but fewer than one percent of the souls in Christendom were wellborn. Typically, the rest—nearly 60 million Europeans—were known as Hans, Jacques, Sal, Carlos, Will, or Will's wife, Will's son, or Will's daughter. If that was inadequate or confusing, a nickname would do. Because most peasants lived and died without leaving their birthplace, there was seldom need for any tag beyond One-Eye, or Roussie (Redhead), or Bionda (Blondie), or the like.

Their villages were frequently [nameless] for the same reason. If war took a man even a short distance from a nameless hamlet, the chances of his returning to it were slight; he could not identify it, and finding his way back alone was virtually impossible. Each hamlet was inbred, isolated, unaware of the world beyond the most familiar local landmark: a creek, or mill, or tall tree scarred by lightning."

was anointed with special oils. These acts symbolized the belief that God endorsed the coming of this monarch to the throne.

In return for the support and blessing of the church, the rulers of Europe supplied weapons and soldiers for military crusades into foreign lands, supported the building of majestic cathedrals, turned over to the church land acquired in battle, and supported the idea of wealthy landowners leaving real estate and other valuables to the church in their wills. By the eleventh century, the church had become the most powerful force in all of Europe and was so tightly interwoven with secular politics that it was sometimes difficult to separate the interests of church and state.

A Wide Gap

It is no wonder that the church guarded its great power jealously. Any idea or criticism that challenged church authority was seen as a threat to the very existence of the institution—and, as a result, to the order of society, as well. In the late eleventh and twelfth centuries, though the church was still riding a crest of power and prestige, resistance was forming.

Some of the rumblings came from individuals who resented the vast gap between the common people, who lived out their days in extreme poverty, and the pope and other church leaders, who spent large sums of money to maintain luxurious lifestyles. Every

Christian paid taxes to the church and was also urged to contribute to Rome's wealth in other ways.

For instance, people were constantly urged by their local priests and bishops to purchase indulgences—in effect, pardons from the church for sins committed. If, for example, a man confessed privately to a priest that he had stolen a neighbor's pig, the priest might offer forgiveness in exchange for a certain sum of money. There are many references in medieval history to peasants going without food or other necessities while using what little money they had to purchase indulgences from the village priest.

Nor did it seem to bother church officials that they were accepting payments to

A medieval European monarch (right) needed the sanction of a church official, such as the pope (center), in order to rule. Thus, by the eleventh century, the church's power was unmatched.

forgive some very terrible crimes. "Selling pardons for murderers raised some eyebrows," writes one historian, "but a powerful cardinal explained that 'the Lord desireth not the death of a sinner, but rather that he live and pay.'"[5]

In addition to criticizing the church's accumulated wealth and its questionable practice of selling indulgences, other reformers were speaking out against obvious contradictions in what the church taught and how its leaders behaved. For instance, although all men of the church were required to swear that they would live in celibacy—that is, they would neither marry nor have any sexual relationships—increasing numbers of priests and monks were giving in to the temptations of the flesh, and many had the reputation of being quite lecherous. In some cities of Europe, "it was not unknown for women entering the confessional box [booth] to be offered absolution in exchange for awkward, cramped intercourse on the spot."[6]

The Cathari

Some people questioned fundamental church teachings as individuals, and simply discussed their ideas with family, friends, or even the village priest. Others banded together, forming religious sects, and tried to gain additional members. The Cathari of southern France comprised one of the first medieval Christian sects. It was the Cathari whose existence—and persistence—prompted the church to eventually begin its Inquisition.

The Cathari were Christians who believed that their lifestyle was far closer to what Jesus intended than that of many modern priests. The Cathari lived simply, supporting themselves on very little money and rejecting the comforts of the material world.

According to their beliefs, such unnecessary luxuries as shoes or soft beds could easily corrupt people. The Cathari helped the poor and tended the sick, and as a result gained considerable popularity, especially in rural areas. As people compared the self-denial of the Cathari with the self-indulgence of many priests and bishops, it was easy to admire the members of the new sect.

By the last years of the twelfth century, it was not only the poor of southern France who admired the Cathari. As the sect became a more visible presence in the region, wealthier citizens were impressed as well. Thus some aristocrats found it politically wise to support the Cathari—at least verbally—since so many of the aristocrats' neighbors and constituents were vocal in their support of the sect.

The popularity of the Cathari at this time was enhanced by worsening corruption within the church, especially in southern France. Not only was the church continuing to sell indulgences, it had recently gone into the business of assigning high church positions,

A page from a book describing a Cathari ritual. The Cathari, who led simple and charitable lives, were seen as heretics by the church.

The Cathari

The Cathari, one of the key sects deemed dangerous and heretical by the medieval church, considered themselves Christian, but with important theological differences. This excerpt from Fernand Hayward's book The Inquisition *explains part of the Cathari belief in two gods—the Good God, and Satan-Lucibel, the Evil God.*

"The Good God created the original chaos and divided it into four elements; then the Evil God . . . seized upon these to create the world. [Satan-Lucibel did not have the power to create the world from nothing.] . . . God having created the world, Lucibel decided to populate it. He managed to get into heaven, and there he seduced to his cause a number of angels. Having lured them to earth, he gave them a body and formed Adam and Eve from the ooze of the sea; then he caused them to increase and multiply. At each birth, Satan draws on his reserve of fallen angels to fit a soul to fit a new body. Thus, for the Christian idea of original sin, the Cathari substituted another notion, that man is guilty because he fled from heaven. Moved by compassion, Good God called together the faithful angels and asked for a volunteer who would descend on earth and bring to men the revelation by which they could be set free. Jesus volunteered, and thus became the Son of God. But since . . . Jesus could have no contact with matter, his body was a body in appearance only. . . . It was Satan who, by means of the Jewish people, determined and secured the passion and crucifixion of Christ; but both the passion and crucifixion were in appearance only since, not having a real body, Jesus could neither suffer nor die."

---

such as the offices of archbishop and bishop, to the highest bidders. Not surprisingly, churchgoers felt cheated and ignored, for many of the new church officials were not interested in their duties as clergymen. Instead of tending to the spiritual needs of church members, they spent their days hunting and visiting with wealthy friends. Scholar Fernand Hayward tells of one new official, Archbishop Berenger, who "thirteen years after his [buying the office] had not yet visited his diocese [official territory]."[7]

Church leaders in Rome viewed critics of the church, especially the Cathari and those who were beginning to support them, as a dangerous threat, and were quick to denounce them as heretics. But heretics were not a threat to the church alone: because of the church's intimate relationship with government, any enemy of the church was automatically an enemy of government, as well.

Treasoners and Heretics

Neither the church nor the government of France had much patience with heretics—called "treasoners" when their criticism and denunciation was of a purely political rather than religious nature. Both institutions sought to separate deviant thinkers from

Corruption in the Pre-Inquisition Church

In The Age of Faith, *Anne Fremantle expounds on the ways in which the medieval church had sunk into corruption. One practice that became widespread was called "simony"—the buying and selling of church offices. Such corruption drew criticism from educated people in France and Italy, soon to be labeled "heretics and enemies of Christ" by the church.*

"The trafficking [of church offices] was two-way. For a suitable sum, an influential churchman would sell a wealthy noble a Church office he wanted for his brother, cousin, nephew, or ally; or the layman, in turn, would sell an ambitious cleric a bishopric or abbey [office of bishop or head of monastery]. The emoluments [payments] to be derived from holding a lofty Church office, and controlling the income from its lands, drew many a covetous eye; and if an aspirant to a bishopric had to pay heavily for his post, he could retrieve the cost by demanding installation fees from his priests in turn. Seeping downward through the ranks of the clergy, cynicism and demoralization encouraged yet another evil. By the 12th century, clerical chastity and even celibacy had become a mockery; monasteries were permitting women hangers-on, and the numbers of priests and deacons who took wives or concubines [live-in girlfriends] had increased.

[One] churchman [who had obtained his office by simony] . . . gave it as his opinion that it would be quite pleasant to be Bishop of Rheims 'if one were not obliged now and then to sing Mass.' Many bishops and abbots found tending their flocks more arduous than hunting, or fathering offspring, or partaking in the ceaseless small wars which marked the times. The lesser clergy followed suit. Dispensing services and charity to the poor became a bore; the priestly obligation to baptize or marry or bury a parishioner was now hedged about with demands for fees."

The consecration of a bishop. Positions in the medieval church were often attained by the practice of simony.

society, although government courts did it in a far more permanent way, often burning heretics at the stake. The church's enemies were usually excommunicated by the pope—that is, deprived of the rights of church membership, a punishment that was accompanied by the stripping away of their property and belongings.

When Innocent III came to the papal throne in 1198, he knew that the church had to stamp out heretics before their influence with the people became too powerful to contain. Innocent believed, as had all popes before him, that the church's most important duty was to protect and support the faith of its members and that this responsibility justified any means necessary to keep heretical views from poisoning what it termed "the true beliefs" of Catholics.

As Hayward explains, "The Church, having the sacred charge of souls, could not permit the faithful to be contaminated by such gross error."[8]

A Triumph for the Heretics?

Convinced of his sacred duty, Pope Innocent III took steps to move against the Cathari. His plan was to get the bishops and other church officials in southern France more involved in their duties, and by doing so, to locate the leaders of the heresy. Once discovered, individual heretics could be captured and punished.

But the bishops found the task more difficult than they had anticipated. While in earlier times a visit from a bishop or archbishop was an exciting, happy event, such public occasions were becoming risky. French villagers, sensing the church's antagonism toward the Cathari, were openly hostile to the visiting dignitaries. Writes Hayward, "If it chanced that a bishop more energetic than

his fellows attempted to preach publicly against [the Cathari], the people rose up against him. . . . One bishop was molested by the Catholics and forced to leave the town."[9]

A Holy War

Realizing that stronger measures were necessary, Innocent III decided to use force against the Cathari. Because the battles would be fought in the name of the church, the undertaking was considered a holy war, or a crusade. The term "Albigensian Crusade" is sometimes used, since the area targeted was near the town of Albi, where there were many Cathari.

News of the crusade spread through Europe, and many responded, volunteering to fight for the church. Soldiers by the thousands came from Germany, from Slavonia (the area that is now Yugoslavia and Croatia), and from Italy. Many were Christians, who saw the crusade as a sacred duty; others were mercenaries, drawn by the idea of looting and pillaging the property of heretics—perfectly permissible, since excommunicated individuals and criminals had no protection from such actions.

The Albigensian Crusade resulted in unimaginable carnage and bloodshed. One of the pope's representatives reported by letter in the summer of 1209 that at one town alone, army troops had forced their way inside the walls and, "sparing neither rank nor sex nor age, slew about 20,000 souls with the edge of the sword; and making a huge slaughter, pillaged and burned the whole city."[10]

The pope was pleased with all the reports of the crusade's success. In a response to his representative's letters, Innocent writes:

God hath mercifully purged His people's land; and the pest of heretical wickedness, which had grown like a cancer and infected almost the whole [area] is being deadened and driven away. . . . His mighty hand hath taken many towns and cities wherein the devil dwelt.[11]

Although thousands of heretics and their followers perished during the crusade, which lasted more than twenty years, many survived. Some escaped to Italy and other lands where the soldiers would not pursue them; others, well hidden by their supporters, were able to avoid injury.

Thus Innocent came to understand that wars and invasions were not going to wipe out all the heretics. A more persistent—and less violent—means was necessary to keep the heretics from coming back and gaining strength once more. As one historian notes, "In order to hold a country it is necessary not only to conquer it, but also to organize it."[12] To finish what the crusade could not, the institution known as the Inquisition was born.

Another Plan

Pope Innocent III decided to send special emissaries to southern France, as well as to other regions known for having allowed the heretics to acquire strong footholds. The papal representatives would become involved in the religious life of each community— preaching and saying mass—thereby providing a more loving, less corrupt model of the church than had been available under the bishops who were behaving badly. Since the whole point of the Inquisition was to help

To eradicate the Cathari, Pope Innocent III (left) launched the Albigensian Crusade, which in turn prompted the Inquisition.

An engraving depicts the death of a crusader during a heated battle with the Albigensians in 1218.

those holding heretical beliefs see the error of their ways and return to the church, Pope Innocent stressed that conversion, not punishment, was the primary goal of these emissaries—the first inquisitors.

Innocent knew that the early inquisitors would be successful only if there were "no unnecessary oppression or cruelty or persecution dictated by private interests or personal revenge."[13] Many bishops appointed before the Albigensian Crusade had been arrogant and corrupt, chiding and scolding the people to whom they preached.

The monks Innocent chose as his first inquisitors, on the other hand, were soft-spoken and kind. They wore coarse robes and went barefoot. They carried no money; when they were hungry, they begged for a little food. The religion they preached was positive and devoid of threats. Messages of hope and redemption, along with reminders that God's world is one of good, were welcome to people who were used to hearing about Satan and the fires of hell from their priests.

The emissaries sent by Rome were as successful as the pope had hoped. The simple ways of the monks were a welcome sight to people who had embraced the Cathari and other heretics as a gesture of rejection of a church often perceived as gluttonous. Many of those who had been impressed by the heretics' ideas now returned to the church. "As [the monks] went to and fro, begging their bread," writes one historian, "they escaped the poor man's envy which dogged the footsteps of the wealthy bishops and the abbots of the older orders."[14]

Adding "Teeth" to Church Law

Despite the success of the first inquisitors at reclaiming lost souls, there were indeed some who refused to repent and continued to criticize and demean the church, no matter how many opportunities the monks gave them to renounce their heretical ways. It was clear that inquisitors whose only "weapons" were love and forgiveness would not succeed against these hardened heretics, who had no intention of changing. It was important, Pope Innocent III realized, to give the church a system for dealing efficiently with these enemies. To come up with guidelines for his inquisitors to punish heretics, Innocent assembled councils of church officials in 1215 to create a policy with respect to persistent wrongdoers.

Traditionally, excommunication had been the fate of heretics. Since, however, the

When Pope Innocent III's humble monks failed to bring all heretics back to mainstream Catholicism, he enforced punishments on those who refused to repent.

Cathari and their supporters were deemed to be so dangerous, church authorities felt a need to add more "teeth" to the standard punishment. After much debate, the council decided that in addition to excommunicating heretics, the church would take more drastic measures.

For instance, heretics would be deprived of rights normally assumed by citizens of that time. Those whose social standing would have allowed them to hold office could not, nor could they appear as witnesses in courts of law. They could not make wills or inherit money from other people. If they were sick or hurt, no one was allowed to help them. "One of the most evil aspects of the ban," explains historian Jean Plaidy, "was that anyone who showed charity to an excommunicated person became himself a candidate for excommunication."[15]

Death to the Heretic?

Nowhere in the guidelines for this inquisition decided on by Pope Innocent III and his council was the death penalty approved for heretics. Innocent had consistently argued for punishments that were strict, yet humane—and these were to be imposed only when repentance and forgiveness were ineffective.

This is not to say that in parts of Europe the death penalty was not handed down—especially by civil authorities who had agreed to cooperate with the inquisitors in any way they could. In Aragon, which is now a part of Spain, King Pedro II had ordered heretics, whom he defined as critics of either the church or the government, beheaded or hanged, declaring them enemies of the state. A medieval king of Italy had ordered that all heretics be burned alive at the stake—after having their tongues cut out, as a warning to others. But these punishments were not considered appropriate by Pope Innocent III.

Gregory IX and Innocent IV, two of the successors of Innocent III, who died in 1216, were nervous about the rising tide of heresy not only in France, but in Germany and Italy. These popes issued edicts that allowed the church to impose much stricter punishments. No longer were the inquisitors' hands tied in matters of unrepentant heretics. By the mid–thirteenth century, the death penalty was an approved option. So was torture, for suspects reluctant to provide inquisitors with requested information. The Inquisition, whose original intent had been to de-emphasize violence in dealing with heresy, was becoming a symbol of inhumanity and violence such as the world had never seen.

By the early mid–thirteenth century the Inquisition operated in a very precise, very predictable manner, following a procedure that—because of its success in rooting out heretics and unrepentant sinners—became standard in every area the inquisitors visited. Papal inquisitors made their way through the countryside, stopping in the towns and villages that were reported to be strongholds of heretics and their supporters.

Rooting Out Heresy

Such visits started mildly enough, with the inquisitor calling the townspeople together and announcing a thirty-day "time of grace" during which sinners or heretics could come forward and confess their wrongdoing. Also during this time of grace, those who knew of others they believed to be guilty of committing heresy or other sins were to report that information to the inquisitor.

Heretics who came forward during the time of grace were usually given light punishments—jail time, or perhaps a pilgrimage to a holy place. Those whose misdeeds—such as adultery, lying, or irregular church attendance—did not involve heresy were given a penance and released.

But when the thirty days were up, the Inquisition took on a more hostile attitude. Suspected heretics who had not confessed were charged and thrown into horrible dungeons. So were people who had been accused by their neighbors—or even a family member—of committing a sin that had not been confessed voluntarily. Only if a sinner or criminal confessed did the church offer to help by showing the path to forgiveness.

Prisoners were questioned for hours at a time—sometimes for days. If they refused to confess, the inquisitors introduced brutal methods of torture. By means of racks that stretched their bodies until limbs and joints

After Innocent III's death, the Inquisition toughened its resolve against heresy, torturing and publicly executing accused sinners who did not confess.

were torn, whippings, and roasting of prisoners' feet slowly over an open flame, the accused were eventually induced to confess—or die. Those found guilty of heresy, those who had once been forgiven but had relapsed, and those who refused to confess were handed over to civil authorities to be killed.

For much of Europe, the public executions, the screams of the tortured, the midnight arrests, and the suspicion and fear that haunted almost everyone became commonplace. Neither a war, nor an invasion, nor a horrendous event lasting a few years, the Inquisition acquired institutional status: it was a grim fact of life.

CHAPTER 2

The Roots of Spain's Inquisition

The Inquisition had been an active force in Europe for over 250 years before it came to Spain. The Spanish provinces—especially Castile and Aragon—were far too involved in other matters to concern themselves with whether heretics lived in their midst. For centuries the Spanish had been at war, attempting to drive out the Moors, North African Muslims who had ruled the provinces of Spain since the eighth century.

By the mid-1400s, however, the Moors had been all but defeated, and two strong rulers, Ferdinand and Isabella, had taken the thrones of Aragon and Castile. Their marriage resulted in a Spain that for the first time in many centuries was united. The new rulers faced difficult problems, however. The

Superstitions in Medieval Times

As explained by William Manchester in his book A World Lit Only by Fire: The Medieval Mind and the Renaissance, *most Europeans in medieval times found it easier to believe in witchcraft and sorcery than in the afterlife mentioned in church each Sunday. A priest who tried to eliminate ancient superstitions would have been considered a fool by his congregation.*

"Although they called themselves Christians, medieval Europeans were ignorant of the Gospels. The Bible existed only in a language they could not read. The mumbled incantations at Mass were meaningless to them. They believed in sorcery, witchcraft, hobgoblins, werewolves, amulets, and black magic. . . . If a lady died, the instant her breath stopped, servants ran through the manor house, emptying every container of water to pre-vent her soul from drowning, and before her funeral the corpse was carefully watched to prevent any dog or cat from running across the coffin, thus changing her remains into a vampire. . . . Nothing in the New Testament supported such delusions and rituals; nevertheless the precautions were taken—with the blessings of the clergy. . . . [I]n pensive [thoughtful] moments they worried. Should the left eye of a corpse not close properly, they knew, the departed would soon have company in purgatory. If a man donned a clean white shirt on a Friday, or saw a shooting star, or a will-o'-the-wisp in the marshes, or a vulture hovering over his home, his death was very near. Similarly, a woman stupid enough to wash clothes during Holy Week would soon be in her grave."

King Ferdinand (left) and Queen Isabella (right) with their daughter (center). The two monarchs ruled a united, though financially troubled, Spain.

financial system was in ruins from the reigns of incompetent and corrupt kings before them; crime was a threat to every traveler; and many of Spain's nobles shamelessly took advantage of the poor people in their districts.

The Jews of Spain

However, the problem that most troubled the new monarchs was neither economic trouble nor murder on the highways. It had to do with Spain's large and prosperous Jewish population. The answer to the question: "What should be done about the Jews?"

would lead Spain and the church to a new sort of inquisition, more vicious and cruel than its predecessor in medieval Europe.

Jews lived in Spain just as they lived in France, England, Germany, and other countries of Europe. It was, sadly, a fact of life that people who practiced Judaism were often treated with contempt by Christians. Jews were called "Christ killers," and legends about "evil magic" their rabbis supposedly practiced were commonplace. England had expelled the Jews from its borders in 1290, and the Germans had led appalling massacres against the Jews "which beggared for fury, system, and comprehensiveness, anything that Europe had yet known."[16]

Spain, however, had treated its Jewish population far better than other European countries. Indeed, Jews had lived in Spain longer than anyone could remember, their presence predating that of the Moors. During the centuries of Moorish domination, the Jews had flourished as nowhere else on the continent.

In the years of what is termed the *reconquista*—the time during which the Spanish were expelling the Moors—many Jews fought in the Christian armies. Jewish businessmen helped finance Spain's military. There was, for the most part, an atmosphere Spanish people called *convivencia*—"living together peacefully."

This is not to say that trouble did not erupt occasionally between the Christians and Jews in Spain. Local anti-Jewish uprisings often occurred because of a rumor—a Christian child kidnapped and crucified by Jews, for instance—or a sickness such as the Black Plague for which the people had no rational explanation. But other than "a few massacres out of sheer habit,"[17] Christian Spain in the years during the *reconquista* was far more tolerant than other nations of Europe.

Changing Status

By the time Ferdinand and Isabella began their rule, however, this harmony had soured. The end of *convivencia* was a gradual process, and historians do not agree completely on the reasons. Some feel the cause dates back to the time of the *reconquista*, when the Catholics of Spain began successfully fighting the Moors. It was true, insists historian Cecil Roth, that "once the Moorish menace was mastered, and the necessity for conciliating the Jewish minority diminished, [the Jews'] position began to deteriorate."[18] Perhaps the momentum of the victories over the Moors resulted in a wave of nationalism, which to the Catholics might have translated into anti-Semitism. After all, weren't the beliefs of Jews as foreign to them as those of the Moors?

Other historians make a case for the difference in income levels of the Catholics and the Jews. Especially in the towns, many people equated participation in financial matters—banking, loaning money, and tax collecting for the government—with being Jewish, and they also noted the high proportion of Jewish physicians, professors, and merchants. Thus Jews held many positions that were very successful financially.

This woodcut depicts Jews being burned alive in Nuremberg, Germany. Unlike other European countries, Spain treated its Jews relatively well, mainly because the country was focused on expelling the Moors.

Pig Pens and Cow Dung

Such success might have impressed the wealthy aristocrats of Spain, but the common people were jealous and resentful. To them it seemed that the wealth of Spain was unjustly concentrated in the hands of the Jews. They had only to look at their own lifestyle, scrabbling out a meager existence on the land, to see that they were far beneath the financial level of many of their Jewish countrymen.

Spain at this time was like Europe had been two or three centuries earlier. The standard of living for most Spaniards, especially in rural areas, was astonishingly low. People who visited Spain from other countries complained bitterly about the conditions travelers faced there. The Spanish countryside had inns, of course, but they were horrible. Robert Gauguin, a French diplomat in the late fifteenth century, was appalled. "I would not even compare Spanish hostelries to French stables," he complained. "That would be doing them too much honor. Even the pigpens of France are better!"[19]

But the filthy inns of Spain differed little from the homes of the common people. Spanish farmers and their families lived in one-

Spanish and Moorish soldiers clash in battle during the reconquista. *Wealthy Jews often financed the Spanish military's fight to oust the Moors.*

Ecclesiastical Map of Spain (c. 1300)

Legend:
- ⚇ Archbishoprics
- ⚧ Bishoprics
- ▨ Non-Christian

Bay of Biscay · Gulf of Lions · North Atlantic Ocean · Oviedo · Compostella · Leon · Pamplona · Orense · Burgos · Huesca · Gerona · Braga · Palencia · Saragossa · Barcelona · Zamora · Tarragona · Salamanca · Segovia · Balearic Sea · Ciombra · Avila · Toledo · Valencia · Lisbon · Badajoz · Cordova · Jaen · Murcia · Mediterranean Sea · Seville · Gulf of Cadiz · Cadiz · Strait of Gibraltar

room huts, made from mud, clay, and straw. (Wood was rare, for much of Spain was treeless.) Many smeared dung on the outer walls of their homes, believing it would draw the flies outside. There were no windows, for glass—common in France and Italy—was almost unheard of in the Spanish countryside.

For fuel the people burned coal, not in stoves or fireplaces, as in other parts of Europe, but in low brazier pits, which were also used for cooking. Unfortunately, poor ventilation often made such braziers dangerous. Every winter whole families were asphyxiated in their sleep by poisonous fumes from coal being burned to warm their huts.

The climate and poor soil conditions made farming difficult, and as a result, food was neither plentiful nor interesting. One historian notes that "the Spaniard ate only to live; certainly he fasted heroically and more

often than the Church required."[20] Meat was almost never seen by most Spaniards, since hunting was done only in the forests of the north. Those who did have meat in their diets used heavy spices to preserve it or to hide the rancid taste as it quickly decayed.

Wealth and Envy

Many of Spain's Jews, on the other hand, were dining well and living in well-appointed urban homes, just like the wealthy aristocrats of the kingdom. In fact, many historians say that it was the obvious difference in the standards of living of many Spanish Christians and many Jews that helped turn the envy felt by the Spanish into resentment toward the Jews. Writes eighteenth-century Spanish historian Rafael Sabatini:

Deluded by . . . the prosperity which [they] had attained, [the Jews] failed to perceive that their accumulated wealth was in itself a menace to their safety. . . . They committed the imprudence of giving a free rein to their . . . taste for splendor; they surrounded themselves with luxury, and permitted themselves an ostentatious [showy] magnificence in their raiment and equipage, and thus proclaimed the wealth they had been amassing through generations of comparative obscurity. Had they confined themselves to this strictly personal display all might yet have been well. But being dressed and housed in princely fashion, they put on princely ways. . . . They allowed their disdain of the less affluent Christians to transpire in their contemptuous bearing towards them.[21]

Poison Fingernails and Tortured Animals

The anti-Semitism that arose in the fourteenth century at first took the form of rumors and gossip. Many of the tales that had been circulating for centuries in the less tolerant nations of France, England, and Germany began to make the rounds of the Spanish countryside. One man swore that Jewish doctors stored a special poison in their fingernails, so that they could kill Christian patients. Another had heard that the tax collectors, primarily Jews in those days, stole half the people's money before it got to the royal treasury.

Many believed that the epidemics of plague, the so-called Black Death that raged through Spain, were the result of Jewish curses. Supposedly Jews also captured Christian children and drank their blood, Jews tor-

tured and killed animals to create magic spells—the incredible stories went on and on. One particular fantasy that never failed to capture the interest of Spanish Catholics centered around a party of Jews

> who had stolen a consecrated Host [communion wafer blessed by a priest] from one of the churches in the town, boiled it to make a magic charm that would contribute to the destruction of Christianity and were so astounded when it rose up from the cauldron and hovered in the air above their heads, that they confessed their sin and were duly burned.[22]

"He Could Not Have Shown a More Fierce or Frothing Hatred"

By the end of the fourteenth century, the anger toward the Jews seemed to be widespread. The number of riots increased, and even Jews who had been most optimistic admitted that their situation in Spain had never looked so bad.

Though many of the village priests tried to stress tolerance and nonviolence to their restless congregations, others did not. Many of the Dominican friars who whipped up the emotions of Catholics in other parts of Europe against heretics now turned their efforts to anti-Semitism. In 1391 one of these Dominicans, Ferran Martinez, raised the fury of the Catholics around Seville to a higher, more terrible, notch.

Martinez, writes one historian, "was a man of little learning, but noteworthy for his indomitable spirit."[23] He absolutely hated the Jews and had been preaching hatred toward them from the pulpit for twelve years. Indeed, it is said that "he could not have shown a more fierce or frothing hatred of them had they been the very men who at the throne of Pilate had clamored for the blood of Christ."[24]

Martinez's message was clear—the Jews were guilty of the most heinous crime in all of history, the murder of Jesus Christ. He told his listeners of the danger in letting Jews live among good Christians in Spain. When he became tired of that approach he attacked the personal habits of the Jews, "which were not considered to be as clean as those of Christians. . . . They cooked their food with an abundance of oil and their persons were reputed to be malodorous."[25] It did not seem to matter which approach he used; Martinez's propaganda of hate fell on ready ears, both in Seville and in the cities to which he traveled.

No Heed to Warnings

As the congregations of Ferran Martinez listened and were stirred by the Dominican's call for the destruction of the Jews, anti-Semitic violence increased. The frightened Jews appealed to the archbishop of Seville for help. Could he not use his authority to stop Martinez from his bigoted, inflammatory preaching? The archbishop was not only sympathetic, he was politically wise. He was, as one historian points out, "not insensible to

A plague victim. Many Christians believed that the plague, or Black Death, was caused by Jewish curses; this was one of the many myths about Jews in the fourteenth century.

The Roots of Spain's Inquisition

the advantages brought to the country by the Jews."[26] He contacted Martinez and gave him a stern warning: no longer was he to use his pulpit to put the Jews in danger of losing their homes and their lives.

Yet Martinez gave no heed to the warnings. He was fanatically convinced that his message was coming directly from God. No one, archbishop or even pope, could stop him from what he considered his holy duty. He

We Ought to Adopt Their Morals

Even though the Moors and the Jews were targeted by the church during the Spanish Inquisition, both groups had added a great deal to the economy and culture of Spain. In The Moriscos of Spain: Their Conversion and Expulsion, *Henry Charles Lea relates how the Moors were admired by the Spanish for their lifestyle.*

"They were virtually indispensable to the nobles on whose lands they were settled, for they were most skillful in agriculture and unwearied in labor. They carried these characteristics into every department of industry, science, and art. As physicians they ranked with the Jews, and when, in 1345, the Prior of the Order of Santiago built the church of Nuestra Señora de Ucles, we are told that he assembled 'Moorish masters' and good Christian stone masons who erected the structure. . . . They introduced the culture of sugar, silk, cotton, rice, and many other valuable products and not a spot of available ground was left untilled by their indefatigable [tireless] industry. . . . In all the mechanic arts they were unexcelled. . . .

Hernando de Talavera, the saintly Archbishop of Granada, used to say, 'They ought to adopt our faith and we ought to adopt their morals.' They were temperate [moderate in their habits] and frugal [thrifty]; they married early, the

girls at 11 and the boys at 12, without fear of the future, for a bed and ten libras or ducats were considered sufficient dowry. There were no beggars among them, for they took affectionate care of their own poor and orphans."

Although Moors (pictured) were targets of the Inquisition, many Spaniards admired their moral lifestyles.

continued his harangues from the pulpit, and if they changed at all, they got worse.

In the summer of 1391 an infuriated mob stormed into the large *Juderia*, or Jewish quarter, of Seville and began a full-scale massacre of its residents. It was, as historian Cecil Roth writes, "an orgy of carnage. . . . Every ruffian in the city flaunted the finery sacked from Jewish houses, or boasted the ravishing of a Jewish maiden."[27]

Baptism or Death—the Water or the Steel

The violence spread to other cities over the next weeks and months. In some places the entire Jewish population was slain—men, women, and children. Mayors and governors, not wishing to see their fellow townspeople murdered or their cities destroyed, often tried to restore order by appealing to the mobs. However, the mobs—sometimes made up of boys as young as thirteen or fourteen— were too frenzied to listen to reason, and "turned furiously against the city officials and forcibly removed them from the way."[28]

As the violence spread throughout Spain, the death toll rose. In the city of Seville alone, four thousand Jews were murdered. Blood ran through the streets of Barcelona, Toledo, Valencia, Cordova, and other places with large Jewish populations. "[Jewish] corpses, stretched in the streets and the squares," testified one witness, "offered a horrendous spectacle."[29] By the time this era of violence was over, more than fifty thousand Spanish Jews had been murdered.

In every city that experienced a massacre, Jews were given a choice by the raging mob: "Baptism or death—the steel or the water." The choice was an old one, the same as that given to the Jews of England, France, and Germany in times past. In the first Spanish massacres, the Jewish response was just as it had been in the rest of Europe—"the steel." Most Jewish men and women chose death over the betrayal of their religion. However, during the butchery of 1391 far more Jews chose baptism than ever before.

Perhaps it was out of despair, for in Spain Jews had felt far more welcome, far more safe, than anywhere else in Europe. If they were to be massacred here, what hope was there for life anywhere else? Whatever the motive, historians agree that the forced conversions of Jews numbered between 750,000 and a million.

Jews and *Conversos*

The violent anti-Semitism died down by the middle of the fifteenth century. The number of Jews in Spain had been drastically reduced: many had been killed; others fled to other countries; many were captured and sold as slaves. A large proportion of surviving Jews had become Christians—known as *conversos*. The rising number of *conversos* pleased the fanatics, even though it was well documented that the vast majority of the newly baptized were forced to submit to the ritual when trapped during the *Juderia* massacres. Besieged Jews finally agreed to the baptisms, as one scholar writes, "combatted with arrows and even more by hunger and thirst."[30]

It is interesting to note, too, that although Rome had strict rules forbidding forced conversions, the pope never invalidated those of the Spanish Jews. The church, apparently, "troubled little about fine distinctions."[31]

The Jews who were baptized found no sympathy from fellow survivors who had staunchly refused conversion. The unconverted Jews considered the *conversos* to be

Jewish refugees search for a new home. Jews who were not killed or forced to convert to Christianity fled Spain.

betrayers of their religion and their ancient heritage. They disdainfully called the new Christians *Anusim*, meaning "forced ones" in Hebrew, and refused to associate with them.

Even though the pogroms and massacres had almost ceased, the Jews who had not been enslaved, murdered, or forced to flee continued to be harassed by the Spanish. Their numbers had diminished, and as a result, the Spanish felt that they could be "controlled" in less violent ways. For instance, many friars pushed their way into the remaining *Juderias*—even into the syna-gogues, where they preached the gospel of Jesus to the Jews.

Long Beards and Yellow Patches

New laws were enacted that took away most of the Jews' basic freedoms. They were not allowed to shave, nor could they cut their hair, restrictions that made them easily recogniz-able as Jews. They could not hold public office in Spain; they could not farm the land;

nor could they be doctors, surgeons, bankers, or tax collectors, or hold any job that would give them authority over the "old Christians." They could not ride on horseback—for that would raise them physically above Christians who were walking. They could not talk or eat with Christians, even those who had been close friends before. Fine clothes, which had once been a source of great pride, were off limits; Jews could wear only the coarsest, least colorful garments.

Particularly offensive to Jews was a law that would be adopted by the Nazis of Germany almost five hundred years later. This law required all Jews to wear on the front of their garments a yellow cloth patch—a "badge of shame"—four fingers in width. "This was not only humiliating," comments Lea, "but dangerous, as it exposed the wearer to insult and maltreatment, especially in the case of travellers."[32]

The reaction of the Jews was one of sadness and increasing hopelessness. One fifteenth-century Jew who lived in Aragon writes:

> They forced strange clothing upon us. They kept us from trade, farming, and the crafts. They compelled us to grow our beards and our hair long. Instead of silken apparel, we were obliged to wear wretched clothes which drew contempt upon us. Unshaved, we appeared like mourners.[33]

From "*Conversos*" . . .

The severely penalizing new laws made numerous Jews change their minds about converting. So many Jews were agreeing to the conversions—although reluctantly—that local churches began complaining about their dwindling supplies of chrism—the mixture of oil and balsam that bishops used in anointing the *conversos*. "It was considered as miraculous," writes one historian, "that the supply held out."[34]

As part of their conversions, the new Christians took Spanish names, dropping their Jewish ones. And as the *conversos* soon learned, the freedoms that had been so rapidly stripped from them as Jews were returned almost as rapidly upon baptism. Not only had they gained back those privileges, they were on completely equal footing with the "old Christians." Within a very short time, *conversos* who had a few days before been oppressed residents of the *Juderia* were able to become doctors, tax collectors, bankers, and university professors. Some even became high-ranking officials in the church! One former rabbi dropped the name of Solomon Levi, became a Catholic priest, and eventually rose to the position of bishop of Burgos.

As the *conversos* reclaimed many of their former professions, their income rose. Soon they were among the most prosperous people in Spain, hobnobbing with the aristocrats and nobility. Many married into aristocratic families as well. In times of economic chaos and political instability during the years before Isabella and Ferdinand assumed control of Spain, many Christians were glad to have the money that a marriage with a wealthy *converso* could bring. Such an idea would have been almost heretical before, but in the fifteenth century intermarriage between Christians and former Jews became commonplace. In fact, within a generation or two, it was very difficult to find a family among Spain's nobility that did not have former Jews in the branches of its family tree. In Aragon, for example, "there was barely a single aristocratic family . . . from the royal house downward, which was free from the 'taint' of Jewish blood."[35]

. . . To *Marranos*

As accepting as Spain's upper classes were of the *conversos*, however, there was a growing feeling among the common people that something was very wrong. In the *conversos*, says Cecil Roth, "they could see only hypocritical Jews, who had lost none of their unpopular characteristics, pushing their way into the highest positions in the state." [36]

And just as before these Jews had been converted, before the restrictive laws were passed against them, the common people of Spain were jealous and resentful. Their own status, their own economic level, had not risen at all. Even though they had always been Christians, in Spanish society they now ranked below the former Jews, and that infuriated them. As the new Christians went about their business on the streets of the city, "the pure-blooded Spaniard would scowl after them. '*Marrano*,' he would utter, with expectoratory [spitting] contempt." [37] *Marrano*, a vulgar Spanish word originally meaning "pig," has over the years become interchangeable with *converso*. In addition to

Spanish nobility of the fifteenth century. Aristocrats of this time often married conversos—Jews recently converted to Christianity— whose money was a welcome benefit.

Isabella's First Engagement

Like many wealthy girls her age, Isabella was betrothed long before she was old enough even to think about marriage. In fact, she had been promised to two different men—her cousin Ferdinand of Aragon, and a friend of her brother's, Don Pedro Giron. She is said to have detested Don Pedro, but was wise enough to know that since the marriage had been arranged by her brother the king, she had very little to say about it.

When she turned 16, young Isabella was informed by her brother Enrique that she would marry Don Pedro Giron. Distraught, Isabella is said to have complained to her closest friends that she would rather die than have Don Pedro as her husband. She worried constantly, lost weight and developed dark circles under her eyes, and took to praying for long periods of time. She is said to have spent hours on her knees, begging the saints to save her from the impending marriage.

Mysteriously, Don Pedro never made it to the altar. En route to the wedding, he was stricken with a violent illness. Four days later, he was dead, and there were rumors that he had been poisoned. And although historians have been quick to point out that Isabella would never have committed a murder, many agree with Jean Plaidy, who muses that Don Pedro "must have had many enemies, and Isabella many friends."

resenting the so-called *marranos* for their wealth and prestige, the Spanish Catholics felt the baptisms had been a sham. They believed that most of the converted had no intention of becoming Christians at all but had accepted baptism only to save their lives.

Historians agree that a sizable population of the new Christians did not fully believe in the faith into which they had been baptized. It was not at all unusual to find *conversos* who either were not completely clear about the choice they had made or who, though outwardly professing to be Christians, kept up their Jewish beliefs and customs. As one historian explains:

[Many *conversos*] took their children to church to be baptized, though they hastened to wash off the traces of the operation as soon as they returned home. They would go to a priest to be married, but they were not content with the ceremony and arranged another in the privacy of their houses afterwards.[38]

Many of the *conversos* continued to make regular gifts of oil to their old synagogues. And although they attended confession at church, they knew better than to admit to a priest that they were clinging to their Jewish heritage; instead they confessed small, unimportant wrongdoings. The confessions were, says one scholar, "so blatantly unreal that on one occasion, a priest is said to have begged one of his clients for a fragment of his garment, as a relic of so blameless a soul."[39]

A Hostile Environment

The envy and jealousy of many of the Spanish "old Christians" became more and more threatening with each passing month. Where once such hostility was directed at

Political Map of Spain (c. 1400)

the Jews, however, the new targets were the hated *marranos*.

The *conversos* had mixed reactions. Some felt very secure in their new lives. They had both wealth and good standing with very influential people. Since they were now restored to being an integral part of the upper class, they were unconcerned. Others, however, were worried about what might develop. Could violence like that which occurred back in the fourteenth century happen again?

Alfonso de Spina

Interestingly, many of the voices most vocal on the subject of *marranos* belonged to people of Jewish descent. One of the most noto-rious was a Franciscan friar named Alfonso de Spina. Some scholars of the Spanish Inquisition say that perhaps he feared that the growing anger of the people would turn against all *conversos*. As a way of insuring his own safety, they suggest, de Spina was "determined to show that he was on the right side by his venomous attacks on his own people."[40]

Whatever his motivation, de Spina was as powerful in his writings and speeches as Ferran Martinez had been eighty years before. The only difference between the two monks, in fact, was that de Spina was not targeting the Jews who had remained Jews. His targets were the *conversos*.

De Spina gave new life to the old rumors about Jews crucifying Christian children or poisoning Christian wells, except in his version, the crucifiers and poisoners were *con-*

versos, not Jews. He labeled them "infidels" and "instruments of the devil," and called for their destruction. According to de Spina, the *marranos* were not just guilty of vacillating in their beliefs, they "jeered at the holy rites of Christianity . . . [and] had merely embraced the Faith for their material good."[41] He called for violence against them, and his listeners responded with attacks on *marrano* homes and businesses. Soon others added their voices to de Spina's, calling for an end to the *marranos* in Spain.

But de Spina and his supporters did not stop there. They would not accept random efforts by the masses to get rid of the despised minority. That was a job that must be undertaken by a highly organized institution. De Spina called for the pope to send the Inquisition to Spain—and especially to Castile—to exterminate those whom he called "false Christians" and to rid the nation of those who were guilty of undermining the true faith.

It was, of course, a very different way to view the Inquisition. The machinery of the institution would not be applied, as its creators had intended in medieval Europe more than two centuries before, to Christians who wished to remain in the church despite beliefs the authorities deemed heretical. De Spina and his supporters wanted to use the Inquisition against people who had converted to Christianity at the blade of a knife, or when tempted by economic and social advantages. They wanted to rid Spain of any persons who, though designated as Christians, were suspected of not truly embracing the faith. It would be up to Ferdinand and Isabella, as well as the current pope, to decide whether such an inquisition was appropriate for Spain.

The Inquisition Comes to Spain

Although there was a great deal of support among the anti-Semitic elements of the clergy for the establishment of the Inquisition in Spain, Isabella was quite set against it. The queen was strong in her Catholic faith—indeed, she was known to be very pious and devout, even walking barefoot to mass occasionally to demonstrate her humility. Her secretary, Hernando del Pulgar, describes her as "a zealous Catholic, and very charitable."[42] However, as pious a woman as she was, Isabella was also shrewd. She could see that most of the hatred against the *conversos* was motivated not by popular concern for the strength of the church in Spain but by envy and hatred. There must be, she knew, better reasons to set in motion the machinery of the Inquisition. The king was also opposed to such proposals.

Strained Relations

Neither Isabella nor Ferdinand was eager to have the Inquisition come to Spain for another reason, as well: the monarchs did not have a good relationship with the church in Rome. Sixtus IV, who was pope when Ferdinand and Isabella came to power, was not as corrupt as many high church officials at that time, but he was certainly guilty of nepotism and favoritism—giving out key church positions to family and friends instead of to the most qualified men. As one scholar writes, "[Sixtus] lowered the dignity of the College of Cardinals by making it a nest of singing birds, a resting place for all his young friends and relations who looked well in scarlet [the traditional color of a cardinal's robes and hat]."[43]

The king and queen had recommended favorite priests and friars for positions in Rome, but the pope had ignored their requests, filling certain positions with nephews and friends instead. This treatment had angered Isabella especially, and she struck back. Threatening to minimize relations with Rome—and also to pull out special royal agents from the Vatican—the queen forced Sixtus to back down, filling the posts in question with the men recommended by the Spanish monarchs. However, the relationship between the pope and the government of Spain was hardly congenial after that.

But many die-hard *marrano* haters were as stubborn as Isabella. They would not give up in their efforts to convince her that the Inquisition must come to Spain. One of the most persistent of these was the queen's confessor, or spiritual adviser, Tomás Torquemada.

Isabella Considers Torquemada's Request

Torquemada was an aging Dominican friar who, because of his strong involvement in the Spanish Inquisition, has been decried as cruel and sadistic by some historians, and whitewashed as "overenthusiastic" by others. According to one nineteenth-century histor-

Pope Sixtus IV (seated) passed over members of the clergy nominated for important church positions by Ferdinand and Isabella in favor of his own relatives and friends.

ian, he was one of those Dominicans who "testify their zeal by a fiery persecution of those whose creed differ from their own."[44] Whatever else he was, Torquemada seems to have been sincere in his beliefs that those he called *marranos* were destroying the fabric of Spanish society and that it was crucial to punish them.

Like many others surrounding the queen, Torquemada, who had known Isabella since she was a girl, urged her to contact Pope Sixtus IV to ask for a papal bull, or edict, that would allow the Inquisition to come to Spain. Isabella respected her confessor's opinions but was at first unwilling to agree. No one around her seems to have known exactly what

she was thinking, for she tended to be very introspective and silent when faced with a difficult situation. Her face and voice, it was said, showed almost no emotion. So self-controlled was she, writes Pulgar, that even in childbirth "she was able to mask her feelings and betray not a sign of expression of the pain which all women suffer."[45]

Switching Tactics

Many of the pro-Inquisition people around Isabella switched tactics, concentrating instead on pressuring Ferdinand. Although the king was not as pious as his wife, he was a good Catholic, and he had hoped to repair the rift between the pope and the Spanish throne. In addition, Ferdinand had a weakness for any plan that could add money to the government's coffers, almost exhausted by the ongoing war against the Moors.

Torquemada and others exploited this weakness by reminding Ferdinand that the crown could benefit financially from the Inquisition. He suggested that Ferdinand insist on a deal with the pope that would allow the Spanish government, not the church, to gain control of all lands and property seized from *conversos* convicted by the special courts.

This idea intrigued the king, who saw the plan as a way to solidify Christianity in his country, as well as being quite profitable for him. As one historian noted dryly, "When the way of conscience is also the way of profit, there is little difficulty following it."[46] Ferdinand added his voice to the others who were convinced the Inquisition was vital for Spain's well-being, and Isabella finally agreed.

She wrote to the pope and asked for a papal bull that would make the Inquisition official in Spain. Sixtus responded on November 7, 1478, with the special order "to proceed to extirpation [rooting out] of heresy *por via del fuego* (by way of fire)."[47] The Inquisition would begin.

Working Out the Details

Although she had been persuaded to allow the Inquisition to come to Castile (the largest part of Spain), Isabella had some demands concerning the way it was to be run. First, she wanted it clear that any land or other property confiscated in the Inquisition would become the property of the state, not the church. This was, of course, a radical change from the ear-

A fifteenth-century painting of Ferdinand II. The promise of monetary rewards prompted his support for the Inquisition.

lier inquisitions elsewhere in Europe; the church had become quite wealthy by claiming the property of heretics as its own. Second, Ferdinand and Isabella—not the pope—were to appoint and control the inquisitors, thus placing the Inquisition under the power of the government, not the church.

Although not happy about giving up either wealth or control, Pope Sixtus IV knew that because the power of the church as an institution in Europe had been declining over the past century, he was in no position to threaten or command civil governments. Noting the pope's hesitancy over granting their demands, the monarchs threatened to recall their envoys and diplomats from Rome. Such an action on the part of Ferdinand and Isabella would make him appear to have no control or authority with the monarchs, Sixtus knew, so he hurriedly—and unwillingly—granted the demands in a written edict, "noting with horror the existence of many false Christians in Spain."[48]

White Robes, Black Hoods

Torquemada, along with the cardinal of Spain, was appointed by the king and queen to oversee the running of the Inquisition in Castile. It was their job, too, to appoint inquisitors as they saw fit. According to the terms of the pope's edict, inquisitors were to be "bishops or other suitable persons learned in theology or the common law, being priests and over

Although Isabella allowed the Inquisition to come to Castile, she demanded that Pope Sixtus relinquish control over the inquisitors and the confiscated wealth to the government.

the age of 40, whom [the monarchs] might replace at will, to have complete jurisdiction over heresy within the kingdom of Castile."[49]

The Inquisition came first to Seville, a large city with a very substantial population of *conversos*. The arrival of the inquisitors and their staff was something of a spectacle, and would be the same in each town or city they visited. They came on foot, an entourage of between twenty and thirty men. The procession was quite solemn, the group sometimes moving to the slow rhythm of a drum.

The inquisitors dressed in long white robes, with black hoods draped over their heads. At the head of the parade was a friar carrying a large white cross. Behind the inquisitors walked a bevy of assistants, among them the Dominican brothers walking barefoot and wearing their trademark coarse, drab robes.

The residents of the towns did little to greet the inquisitors, other than to gather and watch. No matter how critical they had been of *"marranos,"* or how violently they had acted toward them, the residents knew what lay ahead. They had heard tales of the Inquisition. They knew of its terrible power, and the violence that always accompanied it. It is little wonder, then, that the dreary procession into Seville was observed in silence by nervous, fearful crowds.

Fleeing Seville

Some were more fearful than others. Many *conversos* fled several days before the inquisitors were scheduled to arrive in Seville. Some left Spain, seeking peace in Italy or Portugal. Many others sought refuge in other regions of Spain, hoping that some of their wealthier friends could give them protection against the Inquisition.

This sudden depopulation of the area was very noticeable, especially since most of the *conversos* who had fled had been men of property. They controlled businesses and ran government offices as well, and as a result of their sudden departure a great deal of business was simply not getting done. The queen's secretary writes that

> since the absence of these people depopulated a large part of the country, the queen was informed that commerce was declining; but setting little importance on the decline in her revenue, and prizing highly the purity of her lands, she said that the essential thing was to cleanse the country of that sin of heresy, for she understood it to be in God's service and her own.[50]

Although the fleeing of the *conversos* had not troubled the queen, it ended up being a foolish move. For just as in earlier years in Europe, the inquisitors who arrived in Seville believed that if people had left their native country hastily, they must have had something to hide. Suspicion of heresy, in their minds, was equal to guilt. The inquisitors acted quickly; they sent messages to surrounding areas, ordering nobles and other aristocrats to submit the names of any new Christians who had appealed to them for safety. In addition, those *"marranos"* must be arrested and returned to Seville. Anyone who refused to comply would himself be immediately arrested on suspicion of heresy. There were even threats that uncooperative nobles might be excommunicated.

The nobles were quick to comply with the inquisitors' demands that the *conversos* be returned to stand trial for suspected misdeeds—especially the crime of running away.

The Ideal Inquisitor

In his book, The Inquisition, *John O'Brien includes a summary of qualities that would make the best inquisitor. The list was written in 1206 by Bernard Gui, a Dominican friar who was himself an inquisitor during the first phase of the European Inquisition.*

"He ought to be diligent and fervent in his zeal for religious truth, the salvation of souls, and the extirpation of heresy. He should so conduct himself amid unpleasant and difficult affairs that he never loses control of himself in fits of temper or anger; nor on the other hand should he give way to debilitating [enfeebling] sluggishness and languor [weariness], for such torpor [a state of dullness] saps the vigor of an administrator.

The inquisitor must be constant, persevering amid dangers and adversities even to death. He should be willing to suffer for the sake of justice, neither rashly precipitating danger nor shamefully retreating in fear, for such cowardice weakens moral stability. While remaining adamant to [unmovable by] the entreaties and blandishments of sinners, nevertheless he must not so harden his heart as to repel appeals to grant delays or to mitigate [lessen] penances according as circumstances of place and time may suggest, for such procedure savors rather of cruelty. By the same token, he should refrain from too lenient an attitude which degenerates into dissoluteness."

A chained prisoner sits before an inquisitor. Thousands of fugitive conversos *were captured and sent back to Seville by citizens who feared for their own safety.*

As one historian writes, "Such was the terror which the new tribunal had already excited that . . . those demands were immediately obeyed."[51] One noble alone, the marquis of Cadiz, sent back over eight thousand prisoners, an action that surprised his peers because of his reputation for being especially obstinate when it came to taking orders from the church!

Resistance

Some *conversos*, however, had no intention of running away. They strongly believed that the Inquisition was such a bad idea that the monarchs and the church would reverse their decision to establish it in Spain. Reason and good sense, they believed, would prevail.

One such man was Diego de Susan, a wealthy *converso* who was popular with many high-ranking government officials—including Isabella and Ferdinand. So highly regarded was he by the monarchs that when their infant son Juan was to be baptized, Diego de Susan was one of eight men asked to participate in the ceremony.

Susan's initial reaction to the news of the coming Inquisition was irritation, which turned to anger as it appeared that the king and queen were not going to change their minds. Susan and several friends, rich and powerful men, gathered one night in the San Salvador Church, on whose governing body

Susan and a few others served. He spoke to the gathering, appealing for help in resisting the Inquisition in Seville. It simply did not occur to Susan and his friends, writes one historian, that "those pale hard-faced men with their monks' robes and bare feet could not be prevented from changing the way of life in Seville."[52] One witness to their meeting in the church recalls that

> these said to one another, "What do you think of them acting thus against us? Are we not the most propertied members of this city, and well loved by the people? Let us collect men together . . ." and thus between them they allotted the raising of arms, men, money, and other necessities. "And if they come to take us, we, together with armed men and the people will rise up and slay them and so be revenged against our enemies."[53]

Betrayal and a Gruesome Reminder

Susan's strategy was very close to being successful, but he and his co-conspirators were betrayed by Susan's own daughter. Because of her exotic good looks, the young woman was known in Seville as *la hermosa hembra*, a popular term in those days for "a gorgeous woman." She had a boyfriend who was an "old Christian" and, worried in a moment of tenderness that he might be hurt in the uprising, she told him about her father's plan. He, in turn, told his own father, who brought the news to the attention of the inquisitors.

"Nothing," writes historian Cecil Roth, "could have served [the inquisitors'] purposes better, as all the principal citizens of Seville were placed in their power in a single stroke."[54] The men were arrested, tried, and

condemned to be executed. Susan went to his death denying that he was anything but a good Christian.

Overcome with guilt and shame after her father was burned at the stake, *la hermosa hembra* lived the remaining years of her life as a prostitute, wandering from one part of the city to the other. In accordance with her final wish, when she died, her head was cut off and placed above the door to the house where she and her father had lived. The skull, she had said, would serve as a reminder to others never to betray loved ones.

Interestingly, the skull remained for centuries on that building, located on what came to be known as the *Calle de la Muerte*, the "Street of Death." One historian says that "in the middle of the night strange cries of grief and remorse were sometimes heard to issue from the fleshless, grinning jaws." And although over the years it has disappeared, the legend lives on, for even in the late twentieth century Sevillians report that sometimes "the voice of the loveliest of [Sevillian] women may still sometimes be heard uttering shrieks of anguish for her share in the Great Betrayal."[55]

Changing the Rules

Once the Inquisition in Seville was under way, the inquisitors there were so busy after just a few weeks that the king and queen created an extra branch of the civil government called the Suprema to oversee the activities and procedures of the Inquisition. Torquemada was appointed inquisitor-general, which pleased him. However, he was not yet satisfied with the results he was seeing from the work of the Holy Office in Spain.

Torquemada was certain that very many *marranos* were still practicing their former religion in secret. And since they were not confessing voluntarily, their neighbors and friends would have to turn them in. However, laws governing the Inquisition procedure were much the same as civil law: one person could accuse another, but the suspect must know the names of any accusers. The law was very specific—there were to be no secrets where witnesses were concerned.

But Torquemada thought that the system was standing in his way. He felt that although all citizens had been ordered to provide the inquisitors with names of those they suspected, many were intimidated. He and his committee altered the original Inquisition rule; now inquisitors could promise anonymity to anyone who wished to give damaging testimony. As a result, greater numbers of people were willing to accuse *conversos* suspected of having returned to their former faith.

Looking for Pork, Searching for Smoke

To help other citizens of Seville know how to recognize what was termed a "relapsed Christian," Torquemada compiled a detailed list of thirty-seven ways to identify one. Historian Maurice Rowdon summarizes a few of Torquemada's hints:

> If a neighbor dressed well on Saturdays [the Jewish Sabbath] instead of Sundays, if he cut the fat away from his pork [or didn't eat pork at all], it could be that he had fallen back into Judaism. Every man who turned his face to the wall when about to die could be condemned posthumously [after his death].[56]

Torquemada of "Unclean" Blood?

In his account of the life of Torquemada entitled Torquemada, Scourge of the Jews, *Thomas Hope shows that as determined as the friar was to rid Spain of those with "tainted" blood, he himself should have been targeted.*

"But there is one point about [Torquemada's] family that has been generally neglected, a point of considerable psychological interest. Torquemada's blood was not 'clean.' That *limpieza*, or blood purity, of which a high-born Spaniard was so proud, largely because it was so rare, was polluted at the end of the fourteenth century by Alvar Fernandez Torquemada, Tomás's grandfather, who, following the fashion of the time, had married a Jewess recently converted to Christianity. At this time, when the Jews lived in comparative peace and comfort in Spain, before the hideous outbreaks of wholesale murders and pogroms, it was the usual thing for the Spanish nobles, impoverished by the extravagances of life at Court and the petty warfare with neighbors in which they continually indulged, to repair the deficit by marrying the daughters of rich converted Jews, the dowry [money and other property contributed by the bride's family] being assessed high in order to compensate for the stain on the blood. . . . In the case of Torquemada, it undoubtedly contributed to his maniacal hatred of the Jews, a hatred particularly venomous of the Christian sons of Jewish parents."

These were but a few of the signs, and they frightened almost everyone in Seville—"old Christians" and *conversos* alike. Men and women all over town wondered if perhaps something they had done, or had failed to do, made them appear guilty to others. They asked themselves, "Did anyone notice that I did not attend confession last week?" "Did I put clean sheets on the bed on Saturday [as the Jews do], and if so, did anyone see?"

To increase the pressure, Torquemada appointed "inspectors," whose job it was to prowl certain sections of the city, looking for signs of relapsed Christians. They might listen at an open door, hoping to overhear people inside reciting Jewish prayers. They frequently knocked on doors to see whether households had pork in their larders. Since the Jewish faith prohibits the eating of pork, many *conversos* assumed that they could divert suspicion from themselves by answering "Yes, there is pork in the house." Historians say that soon every *converso* home in Seville had an ample supply, regardless of whether the family intended to eat it.

One of the strangest activities of the inspectors was the roof-climbing on Saturday mornings. Friars and other inspectors would take turns climbing to the top of the roof of the Convent of San Pablo looking for signs that a chimney had no smoke, since it is against Jewish religion to light a fire on the Sabbath—no matter how cold the day. From the roof a man could observe the houses of *marranos*. "If he could see no smoke arising from any particular chimney, the house was noted down and the inhabitants were arrested on the charge of keeping the Jewish Sabbath and, therefore, of being [relapsed] Christians."[57]

Torquemada stands before Isabella and Ferdinand. As inquisitor-general, Torquemada pursued "relapsed Christians" with a vengeance.

Prejudice in Isabella's Day

No matter how easily Jews and Christians lived together in Spain, there was always an undercurrent of prejudice. Though sometimes it was silent and unspoken, Rafael Sabatini says in his book Torquemada and the Spanish Inquisition *that such prejudice was never very far from the surface. This excerpt comes from an essay written by a priest before the beginning of the Spanish Inquisition.*

"Just as heretics and Jews have always fled from Christian doctrines, so they have always fled from Christian customs. They are great drinkers and gluttons, who never lose the Jewish habit of eating garbage of onions and garlic fried in oil, and of meat stewed in oil, which they use instead of lard; and oil with meat is a thing that smells very badly, so that their houses and doorways stink vilely of that garbage; and they have the peculiar smell of Jews in consequence of their food and of the fact that they are not baptized, yet the virtue of the baptism having been annulled by their credulity . . . and by their [practicing Jewish traditions], they stink like Jews. They will not eat pork save under compulsion. They eat meat in Lent [a period during which it was traditional for Christians to refrain from eating meat on certain days] and on the eve of feast days. . . . They keep the Passover and the Sabbath as best they can. They send oil to the synagogues for the lamps. Jews come to preach to them in their houses secretly—especially to the women, very secretly. . . . They do not believe that God rewards virginity and chastity, and all their endeavor is to multiply."

Reporting to Rome

By January 1482, the situation in Spain had become intolerable. The anonymous testimony given against the *conversos* was making it easy for anyone with a grudge to send a fellow citizen to jail—or worse. Tension and suspicion were everywhere. Even Hernando del Pulgar, the queen's personal secretary, writes that the inquisitors in Seville, instead of trying to be fair and impartial judges, "showed, by the way in which they conducted their proceedings, they had nothing but hatred for [*marranos*]."[58]

Some of the *conversos*, including those who were part of the Catholic clergy in Spain, escaped from Seville and traveled to Rome, where they hoped to be granted an audience with Pope Sixtus IV. With what one historian calls "a judicious use of their wealth,"[59] the men were granted a meeting with the pope and proceeded to tell him of the plight of the *conversos* in Spain—how "one's enemies only had to make a lying statement to the authorities for a man or woman to have no chance of redress."[60]

The delegation of wealthy *conversos* reported the cruel punishments, the climate of suspicion and distrust. They told Sixtus about the huge amount of property being seized from suspects and claimed by the throne. As the pope listened, he grew more angry at the way the Inquisition was being handled by the Spanish government. The result of this anger was a papal bull, dated April 18, 1482, in which Sixtus IV protested that

> the Inquisition has for some time been moved not by zeal for the faith and the salvation of souls, but by lust for wealth, and many true and faithful Christians, on the testimony of enemies, rivals, slaves, and other lower and even less proper persons have without any legitimate proof been thrust into secular prisons, tortured and condemned as heretics, and deprived of their goods and property and handed over to the secular arm [the Spanish government] to be executed, to the peril of souls, setting a pernicious example, and causing disgust to many.[61]

Backing Down—Again

The pope also outlined changes if the Inquisition was to continue. No longer would witnesses be granted anonymity; suspects must be allowed to have lawyers; prisoners had to be confined in jails, not within the headquarters of the Inquisition. The bull was a brave move, and an important one. As historian Lea writes, "For the first time heresy was declared to be, like any other crime, entitled to a fair trial and simple justice."[62] It must have seemed to the *conversos* from Seville that such abuses of the law were soon to be corrected.

But Ferdinand was furious about what he considered the "pro-*converso*" stance of the Holy Father. In an angry letter to Sixtus, he described the bull as so outrageous he could not believe it was authentic. He mentioned that he and the queen had heard rumors that the pope was becoming lax on the subject of *conversos*, but that "to these rumors, however, we have given no credence, because they seem

In 1482 Pope Sixtus IV issued a papal bull protesting the handling of the Inquisition by the Spanish government.

to be things that in no way have been conceded by Your Holiness." The letter concludes with a thinly veiled threat: "If by chance concessions have been made through the persistent and cunning persuasion of the said *conversos*, I intend never to let them take effect. Take care not to let the matter go further."[63]

Realizing again that his efforts to appeal to the monarchs to hold to church law would be ignored, Sixtus wavered. He suspended the bull he had sent to Ferdinand, and, by doing so, turned over the operation of the Inquisition to the government of Spain, which could thereafter control every function of the Holy Office. The Inquisition was now completely a function of the Spanish government, and the pope—like the Spanish people—could do little more than watch.

4 Eliminating Enemies

With regional offices scattered throughout Castile, the Suprema kept careful account of the activities of the *conversos* and others who were suspected of heresy. Thus every phase of the Spanish Inquisition was under Torquemada's control, and he was able to tighten his grip on the *conversos*.

The results of the Inquisition were very pleasing to Ferdinand, who watched as money and property stripped from wealthy *conversos* poured into the royal treasury. When Torquemada discussed with the monarchs his plan to expand the Inquisition into Aragon, Ferdinand was thrilled. The Castilian Isabella, while caring less about the financial gains to her husband's home province, was eager to broaden the Inquisition's sphere of influence so that Spain could become more united under Catholic rule.

Less Positive Sentiment

The reaction of the Aragonese, however, was far from positive. Some had heard the stories of tortures and executions, and people were understandably apprehensive. "They knew that Ferdinand's greedy hands were itching to seize their treasures," writes one historian, "and when they looked at the gaunt, pitiless face of . . . Torquemada, they would have known—even if his reputation had not traveled before him—that they could hope for little mercy."[64]

On the other hand, many people in Aragon, "new" and "old" Christian alike, had been curious about the people of Castile; they wondered how it was that the people of Isabella's province had put up so little resistance to the ruthlessness of the inquisitors. According to Jean Plaidy, "They must have thought that the Castilians were a little foolish to be as meek as they were, and that they, the Aragonese, would in such dire emergency show a little more spirit."[65]

Therefore, when in 1484 Ferdinand visited Aragon accompanied by Torquemada and

Ferdinand, eager to acquire more money and property, supported the expansion of the Inquisition into Aragon.

two newly appointed inquisitors, many of the assembled citizens were not particularly frightened. The Aragonese had confidence that a cautious and careful attitude would be best, and that if circumstances like those of Castile appeared to be developing, they would take other action. They would wait, and they would watch.

"No Others Would Dare to Fill Their Places"

The people of Aragon soon realized that the Inquisition would be as dangerous in their province as it had been in Castile. In only a few weeks, the inquisitors, Pedro Arbues and Gaspar Juglar, proved every bit as eager as their Castilian counterparts to eradicate heresy. Jails were full, and many *conversos* and other suspected wrongdoers were being tried and executed. It was not only the *conversos* who were angry at what was happening—a large number of the most respected nobles in Aragon circulated a petition demanding that the Inquisition be halted. Their objection was that the government was taking unfair liberties by seizing the property of so many wealthy men—men who "were never allowed to learn the names of those who bore witness against them,"[66] writes Sabatini. Copies of the petition were sent to the monarchs and to the pope.

The despair of the *conversos* was particularly intense as they watched the arrests, one by one, of the most influential and wealthiest among them. Early in 1485 a group of *conversos* met in secret. They believed that since the petition sent by the nobles was ineffective, they had no recourse but to strike terror into the men who were terrorizing them. This could be accomplished by the slaughter of the inquisitors themselves, they told one

another, and "if they were slain, no others would dare to fill their places."[67]

Killing the Inquisitors

The first inquisitor, Gaspar Juglar, died quickly; it was generally believed that someone had poisoned him. Had one of the conspirators gained access to the kitchen where the friar's meals were prepared? No one knows for sure, but the rapid onslaught of severe, wrenching stomach cramps and headache after an evening meal strongly suggested foul play of this description.

Pedro Arbues, the remaining inquisitor, was understandably nervous. "He carefully tested all he ate and drank," writes one historian, "never moved without a bodyguard, and wore armor beneath his habit [monk's robe]; he even wore a steel cap hidden by his hood."[68] But despite such precautions, the conspirators were confident they could get to Arbues—they even chipped in money to create what was in those days a very substantial reward: 500 florins to whoever struck the blow that killed the inquisitor.

It was in September 1485 that the assassins found their opportunity. Arbues was to attend a midnight mass, and six of the conspirators waited several hours in the dark church, "like bloody wolves," writes one witness, "for the coming of that gentle lamb."[69] When at last Arbues entered, it was easy to see that he was taking no chances. He carried a heavy wooden club as well as a lantern. Before Arbues joined the other friars of his order in the chants, he would have to kneel in prayer for several minutes, and it was during this time that the assassins planned to strike.

As Arbues knelt, he momentarily set down his club and lantern. The assassins crept toward him, confident that the chant-

A depiction of Pedro Arbues condemning a heretic family to death. In 1485 the inquisitor was murdered by conversos *in an attempt to end the Inquisition.*

ing of the choir helped drown out the sound of their slow approach from behind.

The first man to strike Arbues only cut his arm, but the second was able to deliver a forceful blow to the head, which broke through the steel cap. A third man pierced the friar's neck, cutting a vein, and the deed was done. The assassins escaped, hopeful that the death of Arbues would arouse the people of Aragon against the Inquisition.

The effect of the murder, however, was quite the opposite of what the conspirators had expected. "The Old-Christians," writes Sabatini, "some moved by religious zeal, some by a sense of justice, snatched up weapons and went forth to the cry of 'To the fire with the *conversos!*' The populace . . . took up the cry, and soon [the town] was in turmoil."[70]

The assassins were apprehended within days, and there would be no doubt about the severity of their punishment. All were killed with varying degrees of savagery, the most painful execution being reserved for the group's leader. This unfortunate man was dragged through the streets to the church that had been the scene of the crime. His hands were chopped off on the church steps, and he was hanged, taken down alive, castrated, and cut into four parts.

Nor was there any doubt that the dead inquisitors would be replaced—Torquemada had two new men in the province within a week, ready to continue their punishments of heretics—especially the *conversos*—with even more gusto.

Targeting the Jews

Yet in Torquemada's mind, it was not enough to rid Spain of "lapsed Christians." If Spain was to be truly united and strong as a Christian nation, it must be thoroughly protected from *all* Jewish influence, whether it was in the form of *conversos* or practicing Jews. If the Jews had not been such a strong, corrupting presence, he reasoned, the baptized *conversos* would never have lapsed. He promised the king and queen that it would be "a glorious day for Spain, when the last traces of the Hebrew Faith had been abolished."[71]

But Isabella and Ferdinand were less sure of this result than was their inquisitor-general. Neither had ever been anti-Semitic; indeed, when some of Isabella's subjects had threatened violence against a Jewish community in 1477, the queen had declared her support for the Jews quite strongly. "All the Jews in my realms," she said, "are mine and under

Legends of a Dead Inquisitor

It did not take long for the slain inquisitor of Aragon, Pedro Arbues, to become a martyr and saint in the eyes of many Spanish Catholics. In his book The Spanish Inquisition: Its Rise, Growth, and End, *Jean Plaidy explains the significance of his death, not only with respect to Arbues's role as a martyr for the church, but also regarding what historians say could have been a turning point in the Inquisition.*

"As for Pedro Arbues, he was now regarded as a saint, and legends sprang up regarding him. The bells were said to have rung of their own accord the moment he died, and twelve days after his blood had been shed it was said (after it was too late to put this to the test) that it was still warm and wet on the stones of the church, and a handkerchief dipped therein would be stained red and provide a holy relic. He was buried in the church beneath that very spot where he was struck down, and a monument was erected to him. He was beatified [designated as "blessed"] in the 17th century by [Pope] Alexander VII, and canonized [declared a saint] in the 19th by Pius IX. But perhaps his chief claim to notice (among those who see the Inquisition as a blot on civilization and an institution which did great disservice to Christianity) is that his death was of significance in the history of the Inquisition. Had the people of Aragon forgotten their enmity [hostility] towards the Jews, had they stood with them against the Inquisition, they could at that time have prevented its growth; they could have asserted their own right to freedom of thought. And if Aragon had taken that turning at that precise time, Castile would surely have followed; and the Inquisition could have become a feeble plant which struggled for awhile and withered away."

Isabella resisted the proposition to rid Spain of all Jews because the government depended on the services of Jewish professionals to run effectively.

my care and protection, and it belongs to me to defend and aid them and keep justice." [72]

At the same time, it was difficult to dismiss Torquemada and his continuous arguments. Certainly the rulers could not accuse the friar of having improper or vindictive motives. Quite the contrary, his strength of purpose always seemed to be "more irresistible by virtue of its purity and singleness of aim . . . he had no worldly ends to serve. What he demanded, he demanded in the name of the religion he served." [73]

But the king and queen were not so single-minded; they wanted not only to keep Spain

free of unchristian influences, but also to keep its government running smoothly, and that sometimes required the talents and expertise of Jews. For instance, both Ferdinand and Isabella relied heavily on the advice and services of Jews at court. Since being targeted by the restrictive laws of 1391, many Jewish men had worked hard to regain their former positions in finance and other lucrative professions. Several worked closely with the monarchs—some as royal physicians, others as advisers on economic matters. In fact, for the past nine years, Jewish advisers had assisted Ferdinand and Isabella in financing the successful takeover of Granada from the Moors. And so intertwined were the Jews with Spain's system of banking and taxing that "unless an impossibly large proportion resigned themselves to conversion, expulsion would mean, if not a total collapse of the fiscal system, at least a considerable diminution [lowering] of revenue." [74]

A Crucified Child?

But Torquemada continued to press the monarchs to expel the Jews from Spain. He spoke of the evils he felt to be inherent in the Jewish religion, stating further that "in spite of all other measures that had been taken to keep Christian and Jew apart, the evil persisted, and was as rampant as ever." [75] He pointed to the rising tide of anti-Semitism among the people—brought on in large measure by the Inquisition in their midst. The king and queen remained unwilling to take the final step of expulsion until one ghastly incident changed their minds.

In 1490 a *converso* named Benito Garcia was arrested with what appeared to be a communion host in his knapsack. It was a sin for anyone but a priest to carry a consecrated

The standard of the Spanish Inquisition. The Latin motto reads, "Arise, Lord, and plead your cause."

host, and so authorities took Garcia before the local magistrate, and then to the inquisitors of the town.

In the course of a grueling interrogation during which he was deprived of food, water, and sleep for days, Garcia maintained that he was innocent of sin, but that he knew other *conversos* who had done something unspeakable. These men had told Garcia, some years before, that they had crucified a Christian child.

It had happened, said Garcia, near the town of La Guardia. The astonished inquisitors sent word at once to Torquemada, who came to personally supervise the Inquisition against the men named by Garcia. In the following months, the men were taken into custody, threatened, and under intense pressure from black-hooded torturers, admitted to the

murder. (It is important to emphasize that confessions thus secured often were false, for prisoners were told the torture would stop only when they admitted the crimes of which they had been accused.)

The men "confessed" that they had taken a four-year-old boy to a cave during Passover and had first made him reenact Jesus' carrying of his cross. They said that they whipped the boy more than five thousand times, and after placing a crown of thorns on his head, nailed him to the cross. When the child was dead, they further stated, they removed his heart, with the notion of performing a magic spell, and buried the remains.

The trial of the *conversos* who had made these shocking admissions infuriated Christians throughout Spain. Although the confessions were coerced and often contradictory, and although no body was ever found, nor any young boy reported missing, the men were executed, "bound to the stake and the flesh of their arms and thighs . . . torn with red-hot pincers, for it was felt that they were too evil to be allowed a . . . quick death by fire."[76]

The Edict to Expel

The news of the La Guardia case spread through Spain, causing violence against Jews to increase as never before. The level of unrest in the country, coupled with the impassioned pleas of Torquemada, changed the monarchs' minds about expulsion. On March 31, 1492, the monarchs signed an edict that gave the Jews in Spain four months to willingly accept baptism or be forced to leave the country.

Horrified, many of the wealthier Jews pleaded with Ferdinand. How could he turn them out of Spain, after they had been so loyal? They begged him to allow them to stay;

they offered to have no contact at all with *conversos* or "old Christians," and promised to serve the crown more diligently than ever before. They even pooled their money and offered the king a gift of thirty thousand *ducats*—a fortune in Spain in 1492—if only he would withdraw the edict.

Expelled Jews Are Beside Themselves with Grief

Historians say that Ferdinand and Isabella were moved by the Jews' pleas, and tempted even more by the gift of money. However, Torquemada passionately persuaded them to remain firm in their resolve. The edict, announced the inquisitor-general, must remain.

Once certain that the monarchs would not cancel the edict, the Jews were beside themselves with grief. Yet many were disbelieving. How could they be cast out of a place they had called home for more than five centuries? It was longer than they had lived anywhere since the time of Moses! Never had they made themselves so at home, and become as intimately involved with a place, as in Spain.

Torquemada urged the Jews to consider the alternatives; he said over and over that he would rather baptize than expel them. Some Jews gave in, but historians say that the large

The Cult of Santo Niño

The little child supposedly crucified by Jewish men near the town of La Guardia caused such outrage against the Jews in Spain that Isabella and Ferdinand were obliged to approve of the Inquisition being established in their country. Although it was never proved that such a child existed, a cult sprang up almost immediately after the inquisitor was able to get one of the accused Jews to confess, as Jean Plaidy explains in The Spanish Inquisition.

"A party of Jews had determined on the destruction of Christianity and that the Law of Moses should be set up in its place. To bring about this state of affairs, they needed to make a spell . . . [for which] they needed a consecrated Host and the heart of a Christian child. These were to be burned to ashes, which, when thrown into wells and rivers, would poison the water, with the result that all Christians who drank of it would die insane. . . .

[The Jews] had found a beautiful four-year-old boy in the doorway of a church, gave him sweets and kidnapped him. He was taken to a cave by night and given 5,000 strokes with a whip. The little boy, runs the legend, bore the beating with great serenity, but suddenly began to cry. This is when the number of strokes had reached 5,000. He was asked why he cried, and astonishingly answered that he cried because they had given him five lashes more than His Saviour had received.

He was known to Christians as Santo Niño; it was said that he was a holy child who was taken straight up to Heaven . . . and miracles began to be performed which were credited to him. It was also said that he had a blind mother who miraculously recovered her sight at the very moment of his death."

majority did not. Helped financially by wealthier Jews, the less fortunate were able to prepare for the journey without the temptation that conversion offered. They worked hard to sell their property and any possessions that could not be carried on the ships. And because they did not know what dangers awaited them, they married off all their daughters, even those as young as twelve, so that they would have the protection of a husband.

Most of the Christians in Spain were quick to recognize their advantage in this situation. Many who owed money to Jewish lenders refused to pay their debts because they knew the Jews had no way to collect.

Others offered very little money and laughed as the Jews, with no time left to bargain or stall, were forced to accept ruinously low prices. Says one witness, "The Jews travelled about offering [their possessions] for sale but could find no buyers, so that they were forced to exchange a house for an ass, or a vineyard for a piece of cloth."[77]

The Frying Pan and the Fire

Exiled Jews, whose numbers ranged from 300,000 to 800,000, had few options. Other countries in western Europe made it very

Prominent Jews appeal to Ferdinand and Isabella's compassion and material interests, but to no avail. The edict to expel the Jews from Spain remained in effect.

clear that they were not only unwelcome as new residents, but also prohibited as travelers from crossing non-Hispanic lands. The only open pathways lay east, to a few cities in Italy, west to Portugal, or south to Africa.

Most journeys met with disaster. In Portugal the refugees were informed that they could stay only six months, whereupon they would be forced to leave. But the worst fate was that of the thousands who had boarded the ships for Italy and Africa. Some died from an outbreak of plague on the ships; others were captured and sold as slaves. Many were lost at sea from shipwrecks. And thousands of those lucky enough to make it to Africa were betrayed by the king of a northern Sahara tribe, who

> after offering them protection, ordered the guard . . . to strip them of all their money and belongings. Having robbed them, [the king's men] violated all the women and girls under the eyes of their husbands, fathers, and brothers . . . [and] ripped open their stomachs with scimitars and knives, having heard of the rumor that the Jews . . . had each swallowed a number of golden ducats in order to get them past the frontiers.[78]

Some of the Jews eventually managed to find homes in Turkey or in the Balkans. Some were well received by the pope and allowed to remain in Italy. Many thousands of the exiled Jews perished, however. Some, counting themselves lucky to have escaped with their lives, struggled to return to Spain, where they eagerly accepted baptism.

Lots of New Enemies

If the people of Spain thought the Inquisition's work was finished with the mass exodus of the Jews from Spain, they were very wrong. It is true that the Jewish population was almost completely eliminated from the regions of Spain. With the thousands of Jews who had returned to Spain begging to be baptized and restored as citizens, however, there would soon be an entirely new population of *conversos*. As one historian points out, "At one stroke the Catholic monarchs had doubled the number of false converts in the realm. Their activities (or suspected activities) would continue to fill the courts of the Inquisition for centuries."[79]

Besides, there were people other than converted Jews to interest the inquisitors in Spain. There were—and would be in the years to come—new targets for the Inquisition. Any Christian who had sinned in thought or deed against the beliefs and laws of the church would be arrested. So would those who practiced sorcery and witchcraft, some of whom allegedly had been spotted by neighbors riding on broomsticks at night.

The Moors defeated at Granada were forced to convert just as the Jews had been, and as a result, many were later brought before the Inquisition for "lapses." And within a few decades there would be new targets of the Spanish Inquisition, such as Lutherans and other Protestants whose ideas about Christianity were considered heretical by the church.

Yet though the crimes for which these "enemies of the church" were being tried differed greatly, the methods used by the Inquisition were identical. They were based on those used in Europe more than two centuries earlier, refined and perfected by Spain's inquisitor-general, Tomás de Torquemada.

Torquemada's goal was to make the entire process more efficient than the old one, as he outlined in twenty-eight articles, known as "the Instructions." The Instructions

An engraving shows the expulsion of Jews from Spain. Although a few managed to find new homes, most perished during the journey or returned to Spain and converted.

explained in detail the way the inquisitors and their court must work in Spain—from dealing with economic matters to questioning suspects and assigning punishments to those judged to be guilty. Just how far the Spanish Inquisition was from the pope's control was evident from one of Torquemada's final articles—the installation of an officer in Rome whose job was to keep the affairs of Spain from coming to the attention of the pope!

Edict of Faith

As in the original Inquisition, people were given a chance to voluntarily present themselves to the inquisitors upon the arrival to their city or town of the pope's representatives. Judges would allow the traditional "time of grace" for confessions, and those who took advantage of this limited amnesty would be granted lighter punishments.

However, as the Spanish Inquisition became more and more powerful—and more permanent—Torquemada all but eliminated the "time of grace." It became more important for the people to help in the detection of sinners, and for that the inquisitor-general needed a means of "deputizing" local populations to be the Inquisition's eyes and ears. This was the purpose of what was called the Edict of Faith, which was a solemn oath compelling everyone who heard it to swear to uphold the Inquisition. The edict was read at various

Martin Luther Speaks Out Against Witches

In Inquisition and Society in Spain in the Sixteenth and Seventeenth Centuries, *historian Henry Kamen stresses that the Catholic Church of the Inquisition was not the only party concerned about the destructive power of witches in the sixteenth century. In this excerpt from an essay he wrote, Martin Luther—himself another target of the Inquisition—speaks out against sorcerers, enchanters, and witches as agents of the devil.*

"I should have no compassion on these witches. . . . I would burn all of them. . . . Witchcraft and sorcery are therefore the works of the devil; whereby he doth not hurt only men, but also, by the permission of God, he sometimes destroyeth them. . . . Therefore the bread we eat, the drink we drink, the garments we wear, yea, the air, and whatsoever we live by in the flesh, is under his domain. . . . Of witchcraft I have spoken before. . . . This vice was very common in these our days, before the light and truth of the gospel was revealed. When I was a child, there were many witches and sorcerers, which bewitched both cattle and men, but specially children, and did great harm also otherwise; but now, in the light of the gospel, these things be not so commonly heard of, for the gospel thrusteth the devil out of his seat, with all his illusions. But now he bewitcheth men . . . more horribly, namely, with spiritual sorcery and witchcraft."

Martin Luther (1483–1546), German leader of the Protestant Reformation and founder of Lutheranism.

times during the year, especially on religious holidays. Its reading was announced a week or more in advance; anyone who failed to attend the reading, the announcement warned, would be fined and excommunicated.

The Edict of Faith was read in parish churches and in the nearest cathedral that same day, preceded by a formal procession: "the clergy marching in . . . the great cross was draped in black, and on the altar two torches flamed."[80] The first part of the edict reminded everyone of the signs of practices strictly forbidden by the church. Since the relapsing of *conversos* was especially sinful in the eyes of the Spanish Inquisition, most edicts mentioned many customs and rites of Judaism. However, there were warnings to be watchful of Islamic practices from the converted Moors and the evil behavior of witches and sorcerers; disparaging comments about the inquisitors were also a focus of attention. The second part of the edict contained warnings about what might happen to people who did not report sinners to the Holy Office.

"Nobody in This Life Is Without His Policeman"

The Inquisition hired informants, called "familiars," whose job it was to gather damaging information about people. It was a familiar, in fact, who noticed in 1530 that a

Inquisitors, draped in traditional robes and hoods, review records. The inquisitors eventually eliminated the grace period for confessions and came to rely on reports of heresy by citizens.

Relapsed Christians

The first inquisitors in Spain's Inquisition issued an edict to the people of Seville. The people were instructed to be on the lookout for those practicing Jewish customs and religious rites and, if they called themselves conversos, *to inform the inquisitors. In his book* The Spanish Inquisition, *historian Jean Plaidy lists some of the ways "relapsed Christians" supposedly could be spotted.*

"The manner in which they slaughtered animals for their food must be observed. Did they cut the throats of the animals including poultry and bleed them? Did they eat meat in Lent? Did they celebrate the Jewish feasts and fasts? They would of course do this in secret, but it was the duty of all good men of the Church to detect them. Did they bless their children by laying hands on their heads without making the sign of the Cross? The law of Moses declared that women should not enter churches for forty days after bearing children. Let the Christians watch for those who respected this law. Let them report any child which had been circumcised or given a Hebrew name. Let them watch for any who took the *Ruaya*, that ceremonial supper before starting on a journey. If in any house a person died with his face turned to the wall, or had had his face turned to the wall by any present at his death-bed, then that house was suspect. If a corpse was washed and shaved and dressed for the tomb, if water was sprayed in houses of the dead, if while mourning there was abstention from the eating of meat, then those who behaved in this way were suspect, because this was in compliance with the Mosaic law."

certain woman smiled when someone mentioned the Virgin Mary, and the woman was brought before the inquisitors. The same fate befell an eighty-year-old man in Barcelona in 1635 when he had a lunch of bacon and onions on a day of abstinence.

Given the worry of being denounced by friends and neighbors as well as by strangers, it is little wonder that daily life in the cities and towns in which the Spanish Inquisition functioned took on an atmosphere of suspicion and distrust. As one man wrote in 1538, "Nobody in this life is without his policeman. . . . Bit by bit many rich people leave the country . . . in order not to live all their lives in fear and trembling . . . for continual fear is a worse death than the sudden demise."[81]

Those who turned themselves in and signed confessions in the presence of the inquisitors *did* receive lighter punishments than those who were reported by others. However, these "light" punishments were harsh enough. For instance, people under these sentences could not wear jewelry for the rest of their lives, nor could they dress in fine clothes—even on special occasions. They could not carry a weapon, nor could they use a saddle when riding a horse or mule. It was made very clear to those confessing wrongdoing that these "light" punishments would last the rest of their lives.

And though those who confessed voluntarily were not required to forfeit their property, they might be called on later to

Young Spanish women are brought before the Inquisition. Those who came forward of their own accord and confessed to their wrongdoings were given relatively light sentences.

give a portion of it to the government. For all of this, they were also expected to be grateful, not forgetting that "they had sinned against Jesus Christ and . . . most mercifully, they were escaping their just due (the fire)."[82]

Those who did not confess—either because they had done nothing wrong or because they were frightened of the consequences—almost always suffered a more dismal fate than being deprived thereafter of fancy clothes, jewelry, and saddles. The alarming process of arrest, trial, imprisonment, and sentencing had been worked out by Torquemada as systematically as the initial steps of the Inquisition had been.

5 Process and Punishment

Those whose names were given to the inquisitors by others had a uniquely unpleasant experience with the Inquisition. Their ordeal began when they were arrested by representatives of the Holy Office, in what some have said was the most terrifying aspect of the Inquisition.

"Like a Bolt from the Blue"

Because secrecy was a key element of the Spanish Inquisition, a great many arrests were made without warning at night. "There would be the sudden knock at the door," writes Plaidy, "and when this was open, the *alguazils* [officers of the Inquisition] or familiars . . . would demand entrance; and if there was any resistance, force their way in."[83] The suspect was not told the nature of the charges against him, nor the identity of his accusers.

If the crime was serious, all the property of the accused was held by the Inquisition until after the trial. If he was found guilty, as usually happened, the valuables would be formally confiscated. Meanwhile, the person's household goods were inventoried by the *alguazils*, and without time for a goodbye to his terrified wife and children, he was led away to the *Casa Santa*, or Holy Office, where the jail and courts of the Inquisition were located.

When a suspect was seized like this, it was almost always a matter of years before the family saw him or her again. The trials

and questioning took a great deal of time— and the courts were invariably backed up with large numbers of cases to be heard. It was not uncommon for prisoners to die while awaiting trial. One man, arrested in 1602 for allegedly having criticized the Inquisition, did not emerge from the *Casa Santa* jail for fourteen years—after he had finally been acquitted!

Made to Inspire Fear

A suspect was first taken to a room in the *Casa Santa* that was almost theatrical in its design, specially made to create maximum fear in the prisoner. It was hung with black drapes and bunting, "presumably to remind him that he was already in the presence of death," writes one historian.

> No light came through the windows; but on a table, which was set at one end of the room and covered with black velvet, there was an image of Christ on the cross, and six lighted candles . . . also a copy of the Bible. Beside this . . . was a pulpit on which there stood another candle; and [here] sat a secretary.[84]

The inquisitors sat at a long table, dressed in their white robes and black hoods, which hid their faces. Their leader, the inquisitor-general, usually did the talking. It was the inquisitor-general who began the

A view of the Inquisition jail in Cordova. Suspects were imprisoned, often for years, in the Casa Santa *jails while awaiting trial.*

questioning of the prisoner, and he who decided how long each interrogation session would last.

Interrogation was a grueling process, for the inquisitors were well trained in rhetoric, or expressing themselves verbally. Prisoners were often uneducated and could not keep up with the rapid-fire questions posed by the inquisitors. Many an innocent suspect became ensnared in word traps set by the inquisitors and incriminated himself. A secretary sat in at every interrogation, not only taking down the words of the suspect, but recording his gestures and mannerisms as well. Anything that might indicate that the suspect was lying would be noted—trembling, stuttering, even a nervous twitch of the eyebrow.

It *was* possible—although highly unusual—for a prisoner to be freed after the initial questioning. If, for instance, the inquisitors became convinced that a person had been denounced by individuals with petty personal grudges, that prisoner usually was released. On those rare occasions, the inquisitors needed to make absolutely certain that the secrecy of the Inquisition was maintained. That is why anyone released who spent any amount of time at the *Casa Santa* had to take an oath, "to preserve silence as to all they had done, seen, or heard . . . or incur a penalty of 100 or 200 lashes."[85]

Guilt Was Assumed

Unlike many countries of the world today, where a defendant is presumed innocent until proven guilty, those arrested by the Inquisition were assumed to be guilty.

Inquisitors were warned not to be moved by what sounded like genuine protestations of innocence, nor tempted to feel pity for the people they questioned. Such emotions would surely result in failure to achieve the ultimate goal.

The inquisitors were told to remember that they were not doing their job out of anger or hatred. Quite the contrary, they believed that their function was to save the souls of sinners and heretics, most of whom did not understand how much their souls needed saving. It was the Inquisition, propo-nents believed, that "would endeavor to save [sinners] from themselves, set them on the right path and so bring them to salvation instead of letting them slide into the sul-phurous fires of hell."[86]

Because everyone who came before the court was presumed to be guilty, the idea was not to decide whether a given defendant had or had not committed a crime but to secure a conviction. Interrogations lasted for hours. If a suspect continued to maintain his or her innocence, the inquisitors would suspend the session while the prisoner was taken in chains

Inquisitors were interested only in convicting defendants in order to "save their souls"; they assumed guilt and showed no sympathy for the accused.

to a dark, dank cell, usually in the basement of the *Casa Santa*, to await the next session. The inquisitors used the time to study the secretary's notes and look for contradictory statements to exploit later.

The following sessions were more frightening still. The questions came faster and the voices were louder, and the weary prisoner could hardly make proper responses. If, after several sessions, a prisoner refused to confess, the inquisitors used trickery. They returned the person to the jail but placed a spy in a nearby cell. Posing as a prisoner of the Inquisition, over several days the spy tried to gain the trust of the suspect. Later, of course, the spy reported to the inquisitors anything the suspect had said that might point to the suspect's guilt. If, after many grueling interrogation sessions the prisoner had not confessed, the inquisitors proceeded to the next step, as outlined in Torquemada's Instructions. Although this step consisted of torture, in many creative and ugly forms, it was known to the agents of the Inquisition euphemistically as "the Question."

For a Prisoner's Own Good

In the same way they justified their methods in the long interrogation sessions, the inquisitors saw nothing unchristian in the practice of torturing prisoners. "In most instances," explains one scholar, "torture was imposed only to induce the prisoner to confess what the Inquisitors already knew, for . . . unless he confessed fully, penitence was impossible, and the result was damnation to the soul."[87] According to Torquemada, "saving" a prisoner's soul was far more crucial than any other

A Relic Speaks

In his book The Inquisition, *John O'Brien describes a steel torture chair from a city near Valencia. The device is now on display in a London museum.*

"It includes a movable seat, with pinion and rack, manacles [shackles] for feet and hands and, most unusual of all, a skeleton-helmet with screws to put pressure on the top of the head, to pierce the ears and to torture the nose and the chin.

In addition, there is a gag for the mouth with rack-action for forcing the mouth open and dragging forward the tongue, screw-forceps for extracting toenails, single and double thumbscrews, and various other padlocks, buckles, chains, keys and turn-screws. Excavated with the chair was a steel whip, having eight thongs, each of which ends in a blade. Engraved on the mouth-gag are the words 'Santo Oficio Caballero' —the noble Holy Office, namely the Inquisition, and the date 1676. What a monument to the Roman Congregation in charge of the Inquisition.

Standing before that barbarous instrument, which sought to torture virtually every nerve in the victim's body, the spectator is afforded a glimpse into the incredible savagery with which the Spanish Inquisition sought to eradicate all so-called heretics and impose the Catholic faith upon Moors and Jews."

A woman, wearing a miter hat for humiliation, is strangled. The Inquisition saw torture as a way to get the accused to confess, not as the resulting punishment for a transgression.

end; therefore his Instructions put more emphasis on the use of torture than did the laws governing the first Inquisition.

It would be wrong to judge the Spanish Inquisition solely on the grounds that its agents frequently tortured people, for the criminal courts of Spain and other European countries of the day also handed down penalties of extreme cruelty. Cutting off arms and legs, beheading, and hanging were all standard forms of punishment for crimes such as stealing, rape, and murder. The secular courts, however, did not use torture to force prisoners to confess. For the inquisitors, torture was not a punishment, but a means to an end.

Sometimes, the mere threat of torture was enough to make a prisoner confess. Other prisoners who initially refused to confess changed their minds when they were strapped into an instrument of torture. But for those who were extraordinarily courageous, it was necessary to impose a question in the most painful way possible.

Hoisting and Gagging

The inquisitors were present at the torture sessions, so that when the pain became unbearable and a victim confessed, these court officials could hear firsthand the admission of guilt. However, the inquisitors did not administer the torture; local public executioners did the dirty work, earning either a little extra money or a special blessing from the church.

One of the most frequently used forms of torture was called the hoist. A prisoner's hands

Inquisitors commence the hoist, a torture that often ripped the arms from their sockets. A secretary waits, pen poised, in anticipation of a confession.

were fastened behind him and held securely by a long rope, which was strung through a pulley attached to the ceiling. The prisoner was raised off the ground by the rope, so that his whole weight was supported by his arms. By this means, writes an eighteenth-century witness, "he is put to the most exquisite pain, and is forced to cry out in a terrible manner."[88] For several minutes the prisoner dangled, shrieking in pain; then he was lowered to just a few inches off the ground, where weights were fastened to his legs. Then he was raised up to the ceiling again.

Torture on the hoist was excruciatingly painful, and it was very common for a prisoner's arms to be yanked from their sockets, both because they could not support his body weight and as a result of the jerky manner in which he was lowered and raised on the rope. A prisoner who passed out from the pain was lowered and carried to his cell. One rule of the Inquisition stated that a prisoner could not be tortured more than once, but inquisitors got around this provision by merely "suspending" the torture until a prisoner who had passed out regained consciousness.

The water torture, known as the *potro*, was one of the most cruel in the repertoire of the Spanish Inquisition. The prisoner was placed on a wooden structure resembling a ladder, with his head angled slightly lower than his legs. His head was held secure by a tight metal band around his forehead, and arms were restrained by tight cords, so that any struggling at all would result in painful cuts in the skin. Then his mouth was forced open with a metal prong, his nostrils plugged, and a piece of white linen placed across his open jaws. Water was poured slowly onto the linen, forcing the cloth deeper and deeper into the victim's throat. As water filtered through the cloth, writes Sabatini, "the patient was subjected to all the torments of suffocation, the more cruel because he was driven by his instincts to make futile efforts to ease his condition."[89] The prisoner's instincts were, of course, to swallow, yet as he did so, it felt to his burning lungs as though he were suffocating.

Occasionally the torturers pulled up the linen from deep in a victim's throat, and with it came water and a great deal of blood, which "put ye unhappy wretch into the ago-nies of death."[90] The inquisitors, as always, were standing near, to see whether the subject was ready to make a confession. If not, more water was forced down his throat, and the ordeal went on. The longer the *potro* continued, the more likely it was that the water-soaked linen would cause asphyxiation, followed by pulmonary hemorrhage and an excruciatingly painful death.

It is interesting to note that although the rules of the Inquisition prohibited the inquisitors and torturers from prolonging *la question* to the point of death, fatalities frequently happened anyway. For that reason the inquisitors safeguarded their consciences by making a formal statement beforehand, declaring that if the victim were to die, it would not be the fault of the inquisitor, but of "the culprit himself, who

A victim of the potro *suffocates as water is poured through linen into his mouth, forcing the cloth down his throat.*

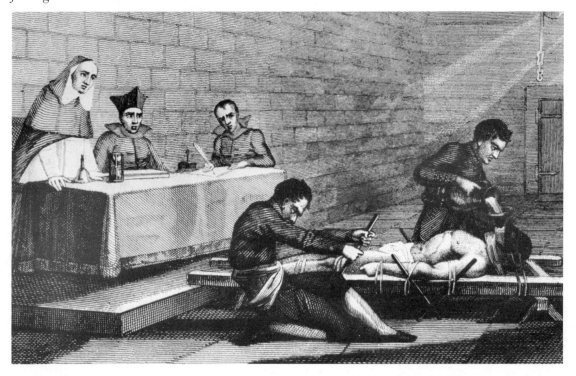

had failed to take the opportunity to tell the truth spontaneously."[91]

Roasting Feet and Frightened Mice

There were no restrictions on age or sex when it came to torture. Not even pregnant women were spared the Question, although some torturers permitted women to undergo their ordeals in a sitting position. Otherwise, girls and boys barely twelve years old, as well as men and women in their eighties and nineties, were tortured as enthusiastically as anyone else. One recorded case in Seville documents a 96-year-old woman who died soon after being whipped and tortured on the hoist.

Some of the inquisitors in Spain were inventive in their methods, say historians. There are reports of prisoners held in chairs by belts while their feet were roasted over a fire. To make the flesh burn more slowly, and thus more agonizingly, torturers smeared grease or fat onto the feet. The ancient device called the rack was used to stretch prisoners' muscles and ligaments—often to the point of pulling arms and legs from their sockets. Frequently, those who survived the rack were so crippled they never walked again.

One account of a torture used in Toledo involved trapping several mice in an upside-down bowl, placed on the naked stomach of a prisoner. Torturers then heated the bowl. As the vessel became hotter and hotter, the fran-

Turning the Tables on the Inquisitors

In The Spanish Inquisition, *historian Cecil Roth relates an incident in which a Christian noble who was very much opposed to the institution showed an inquisitor first-hand just how meaningless confessions under torture actually were.*

"Torture was potentially a double-edged weapon; and it may be imagined that had the same methods been applied to the inquisitors as the latter applied to their victims, the results would have been very similar. On one occasion, indeed . . . the experiment was tried. The physician of a certain powerful Portuguese noble was arrested by the Holy Office on the charge of being a Judaizer [secret Jew]. His employer wrote to the inquisitor, giving his personal assurance that the accused was as good a Christian as himself. The reply came that the prisoner had confessed his crime under torture. . . . The noble, greatly incensed, invited the inquisitor to dinner. Afterwards, he had his guest seized by his servants, and amused himself by practicing on him the preliminaries of a few favorite Inquisitional torments. The victim was able to escape only after signing with his own hand a declaration that he, too, was a secret Jew. . . . One is to imagine, presumably, an exchange of confessions, followed by the acquittal of the accused; but it is not altogether impossible that the inquisitor's admissions were actually founded on truth. For it is obvious that the evidence extracted under torture shows a depressing tendency to reveal precisely what the judges desire and expect, whether true or false."

A torture session of the Inquisition, including (from left to right) the roasting of a defendant's feet, the potro, *and the hoist. Various instruments of torture, including whips with blades on the ends, hang on the wall.*

tic mice, realizing that they could not escape, "burrowed into the flesh of the sufferer."[92]

As during the initial interrogations, a secretary was present at all torturing sessions. It was his job to write down not only the prisoner's words, "but all of his shrieks, cries, lamentations, and appeals for mercy,"[93] as one scholar remarks. It is those details that make such records even more chilling to read, as in the case of a woman named Elvira de Campo, who had been brought before the Inquisition because it had been reported that she did not eat pork.

De Campo admitted to a pork-free diet, but denied that she had any heretical intent, saying simply that pork made her sick. After several torture sessions involving the *potro*, she begged her torturers to tell her what to

confess. Here is a small portion of the secretary's record of one of those sessions:

> If I knew what to say, I would say it. Oh, señor, I don't know what I have to say— oh, oh, they are killing me—if they would tell me what to say—Oh señores!—Oh, my heart! . . . [The linen was brought up from her throat.] Take it away, I am strangling, and am sick in the stomach . . . [another jar was poured down her throat].[94]

The woman's confession was not specific enough for the inquisitors, who demanded more details. She was made to endure several more torture sessions, in which she was stripped naked and bound to the rack. The torturers allowed four days to go by between

"Tell Me What I Have to Say"

It is difficult to know whether the torture applied by the inquisitors forced truthful confessions, or whether victims were simply in so much pain that they would say anything to stop it. This excerpt from Cecil Roth's The Spanish Inquisition *is a word-for-word account by an inquisition secretary of a torture session of a woman named Elvira de Campo, in 1567.*

"She was carried to the torture chamber, and told to tell the truth, when she said she had nothing to say. She was ordered to be stripped and again admonished, but was silent. When stripped she said, 'Señores, please God, I have . . . done nothing.' She was told . . . to tell the truth. The tying of the arms commenced . . . she screamed and said, 'Tell me what you want, for I don't know what to say.' She was told to tell what she had done, for she was tortured because she had not done so, and another turn of the cord was ordered. . . . She said, 'Loosen me a little, that I might remember what I have to tell; I don't know what I have done; I did not eat pork for it made me sick; I have done everything; loosen me and I will tell the truth.' Another turn of the cord was ordered, when she said . . . 'Señor, I did not eat it because I did not wish to.' . . . She was told to tell what she had done contrary to our holy Catholic faith. She said, 'Take me from here and tell me what I have to say—they hurt me— Oh, my arms, my arms!' which she repeated many times and went on, 'I don't remember—tell me what I have to say— Oh wretched me! I will tell all that is wanted, Señores—they are breaking my arms—loosen me a little—I did everything that they say of me.'"

sessions, writes one historian, "so that the limbs would have time to stiffen, so that repetition became all the more painful." [95]

Pain and Humiliation

Many prisoners confessed during torture and were put back in their cells overnight. It was important to the Inquisition that all confessions it accepted be genuine, so each person who confessed on one day had to appear before the court on the next day, to hear the reading of a transcript of his words. If the prisoner took back his confession, the torture was resumed; if the prisoner confirmed the accuracy of the confession as read, he signed the written copy and was assigned a punishment.

Those who confessed were punished severely but avoided being burned at the stake. Even so, some of the punishments were so horrendous that many who received them were scarred for life, both emotionally and physically.

Some were exiled from Spain for a given number of years, or even for life. Their families were forbidden to have any contact with them, lest they draw suspicion of wrongdoing on themselves. Some were sentenced to public whippings on a regular basis. One man in Barcelona was forced to sit naked on a mule and be paraded up and down the roads of the city each Friday, for two years. Spectators were encouraged to approach and whip the animal's passenger across the back and shoulders.

In another case, a young boy whose "crime" was having been sexually molested by a priest was forced to wear an elaborate hat made of feathers while being whipped first by people who lined the city streets as he walked slowly to the public whipping site, and then by the official torturer. The boy died in the course of his second whipping; the priest was not punished.

Another dreaded punishment was wearing a garment called the *sanbenito*, a bright yellow robe decorated front and back with a black cross, and also bearing the wearer's name. A miter hat—one in the shape of a bishop's headgear—was worn, too. The *sanbenito* had been used and then abandoned during the Inquisition in Europe. Church leaders thought that the humiliation and ridicule endured by the wearer were far too harsh:

> The multitude spared neither insults nor mockery to those who bore this token of salvation [the cross] as a sign of infamy. They were pointed at with the finger of scorn; men avoided their company and refused all alliance with them and their children.[96]

Torquemada not only revived the *sanbenito* for the Spanish Inquisition, he extended its use. Some confessed heretics were sentenced to wear it each Sunday for a year or two; others wore it every day for the rest of their lives. Death was no release,

The fire torture. If a defendant confessed to a misdeed during torture, and did not revoke the confession later, a sentence was then handed down.

either—when the wearer died, the *sanbenito* bearing his or her name was hung in the person's parish church, as a warning to the descendants and a reminder of the family's shame.

The *Auto-da-Fé*

Prisoners who suffered threats, tortures, and imprisonment yet did not confess were burned at the stake. The inquisitors could not directly sentence a prisoner to death, for the rules of the Inquisition did not allow that. Rather, the inquisitors "released" such prisoners to the secular arm of the government—the civil courts—which could be relied on to pass and carry out a sentence of execution.

This "releasing" of the prisoners—called an *auto-da-fé*, or "act of faith"—occurred once every four weeks or so at the height of the Inquisition in Spain, less often after that. The ceremony was a very public spectacle, held in a city's large open square. It was directly following *auto-da-fé* that prisoners scheduled for death were burned at the *quemadero*, or "burning place," just outside the city limits.

The gruesome *autos* were well attended. Many drew between 8,000 and 10,000 people, and one in Seville in 1660 had over 100,000 in attendance. Spectators were definitely encouraged—the church promised forty-day indulgences for all who attended, and even more blessings for those who brought wood to stoke the fires at the *que-*

Prisoners wearing sanbenitos *and miter hats stand with their hands nailed to posts during an* auto-da-fé—*the releasing of defendants to the civil court for execution.*

maderos. The crowds that came from other places to witness the *autos* were so thick that usually "the vast expanse of the [field around the square] was one dense mass of coaches, horses, and human beings, none of whom could move until the whole affair was over."[97]

An *auto-da-fé* ran from dawn to early evening. The spectacle started with a solemn parade, in which inquisitors, executioners, and civil and church authorities marched slowly and silently to the public square. The prisoners marched, too—wearing special *sanbenitos* with flames and hideous monsters and devils drawn on them, to illustrate what awaited the condemned souls.

Dead Bodies and Rowdy Crowds

One of the most horrible sights of the march was the procession of men carrying dead bodies bound for the fire. Some of these had died during torture or imprisonment; most were people who were tried and convicted long after their deaths. The corpses of these were dug up and would be thrown into fires, too. The stench and sight of the decayed bodies, many with muscle and skin still attached, must have been unspeakably hard on the families of the deceased. "What a strange spectacle," writes one scholar, "found in no other court in the civilized world, is the spectacle of a vengeance which reaches into the grave to exhaust its fury . . . against a person whose soul has passed beyond the inquisitor's reach."[98]

A mass was said by a local priest, and then began the long business of the inquisitors' reading of the crimes of each prisoner. Often the crowd became restless and rowdy during this part, and sought amusement by tormenting the prisoners, who were sitting in the stands near the spectators. Members of the audience would boo and throw things, sometimes grabbing several *converso* prisoners and roughly shaving their beards—a ritual that delighted many onlookers.

To the *Quemadero*

At the end of the formal ceremony, those destined to be burned were strapped to the backs of mules, which slowly made their way to the *quemadero*. Here a white cross was set up, amid as many stakes as would be needed—sometimes more than fifty in a day. Under each stake was a bundle of wood and enough kindling to ensure a hot fire.

Prisoners were tied to stakes, and before the burning began, they were asked once again if they would like to be reconciled with God. Mercy would be shown to them, a priest promised, for it was never too late to confess. However, anyone tied to a stake who thought that "mercy" meant that his life would be spared was wrong. The Inquisition's idea of mercy at this stage was to strangle a condemned prisoner before the fire was lit—and indeed, when the torch was lit, some prisoners begged for the quicker death.

The lighting of the torch was a prestigious job, assumed by a visiting dignitary. (Many, especially those who had never witnessed an *auto-da-fé* and did not know what to expect, became ill and declined the honor.) Once lit, the torch was used to set fire to the wood beneath the first stake, and the execution was begun. If the organizers of the *auto* were honored by the presence of a member of the Spanish monarchy, they would hand to him or her a little piece of kindling with a bunch of green ribbons (green was the official color of the Inquisition in Spain) to toss on the blaze.

A crowd gathers at the quemadero *to watch as the condemned are engulfed in flames and burned alive.*

After the last of the victims was dead, their ashes were scattered in the fields and in the rivers, so that no trace of them would exist. The *sanbenitos*, which had been removed before the prisoners were burned, were sent to their respective parish churches for permanent display. The scaffolding that had been set up in the square to accommodate the large crowds was not removed, however, since another *auto* would most likely be held soon. And the people of the city, though exhilarated by the events of the day, would see that scaffolding on their way to market the next day and be tormented by a nagging worry: Who would be the next to die?

A Gradual Demise

The Inquisition held authority in Spain for over 350 years, long outliving the monarchs who approved its establishment as well as the inquisitor-general who was its real creator. Its officials and judges continued to punish and execute those it thought to be dangers to "the Christian society of Spain." As the Inquisition continued, it expanded past its original boundaries, casting its net into other places to find enemies.

The Inquisition Spreads to the New World

As Spain acquired new landholdings in Central America and South America, the Inquisition took up residence in the New World. Many Jews eventually emigrated there, seeking a peaceful place to live and work after their expulsion in 1492. However, when the Spanish explorers arrived—and not far behind them, the Inquisition—the Jews were the first targets.

The Inquisition operated in the New World very much as it did in Spain. Those who were Jews were given a specific number of days to convert or leave; after that they would be arrested. Spies were employed to watch *conversos*, and those believed to be "lapsed" were punished, and sometimes condemned to death. The most severe punishments went to Jews and "lapsed" Christians, as well as to non-Hispanic European traders and explorers who were Protestants.

"The Cemetery of Literature"

Another new territory for the Inquisition was the prohibition of certain books that inquisitors found heretical and therefore offensive. The reasoning was consistent with that justifying the Inquisition—if listening to heretics and sinners was sinful, was it any less sinful to read their words?

The censorship of books began in the mid–sixteenth century, and continued well into the nineteenth. Thousands of books were destroyed, or had passages crudely marked out with ink, all in the name of keeping Spain safe from dangerous ideas. All over the country, booksellers were forced to turn over inventory that had been declared evil. Private collections were seized, and even incoming ships were delayed at ports while officials searched their cargo for contraband books.

The books thought to be the most dangerous were usually foreign, for east of the Pyrenees, Europe was enjoying a rebirth of literature and philosophy. Just as Spain had been isolated from the rest of Europe in the fifteenth century because of its long war with the Moors, it was cut off again when its people were forbidden to read what was going on in the rest of the world. Spain was, says one historian, "the cemetery of literature."[99]

Science, philosophy, art—these were all suspect if they in any way contradicted what the church believed to be truth. Even the Bible was banned for many years in Spain because inquisitors felt that certain passages

The landing of Columbus in the New World. Along with the Spanish explorers came the Inquisition, which targeted Jews who had fled to the New World, relapsed Christians, and Protestants.

could be misinterpreted by people who lacked advanced education in theology. The Inquisition was so convincing in its arguments, in fact, that for several generations people either were ignorant that the Christian scriptures existed or, if they knew of the Bible, were in horror of it. It was "a strange state of things," says historian Charles Gorham, "in a country where piety was more common than bread and butter."[100]

Limpieza de Sangre

Spain continued to batter its *converso* population, not only by trying to prove them to be Judaizers, but by passing and enforcing legislation known as the *limpieza de sangre*, or "purity of blood," laws. So hated were the Jews and Moors in Spain that in the sixteenth century laws were passed requiring anyone with any "taint" of Jewish or Moorish blood to be banned from seeking office, or from marrying a true Christian.

The Inquisition kept meticulous records of family bloodlines, and before a person could seek office or marry, registrars checked back four or five generations to make sure the party had *limpieza*. Many families who were proud of their "untainted" blood bought special certificates to verify themselves as pure Christians. On the other hand, those who were not certain of their bloodlines feared the repercussions of being even a little Jewish or Moorish and opted not to find out through the government. There was even a large part of the population who chose not to marry, to avoid the necessary process of documentation. "Women entered nunneries and men remained celibates rather than run the risk,"[101] explains one historian.

Not an Abrupt End

The Inquisition *did* end in Spain, although its demise occurred in stages, over many years, and for varying reasons. One was the gradual irritation of educated people over the constant harassment. People were weary of being accused, weary of being questioned about what books they or their friends read.

Much of this irritation stemmed from the changes that became visible within the Inquisition itself by the middle of the eighteenth century. Despite its origins in Spain due to what many people then agreed was a noble idea—fighting heresy and protecting the Christian faith—the Inquisition had become corrupt and arrogant. Inquisitors seemed far more interested in making money than in preserving the faith. They took bribes, broke

The burning of books in a Spanish church. In the mid–sixteenth century the Inquisition banned books that it found to be heretical; the practice continued into the nineteenth century.

rules that were enforced for other people, and generally acted as though they were above the law. Many inquisitors and their staffs had mistresses; some had children—although as priests or monks they were supposed to be celibate.

The inquisitors had always received a share of the money confiscated from prisoners, but these spoils had decreased greatly since the early years of the Inquisition because most of the wealthy citizens had already been brought before the courts and had their property confiscated. The book bans had been time-consuming and costly, and with less money in their budget—and less cooperation from some of the monarchs following Ferdinand and Isabella—the inquisitors often resorted to bribery. Such actions by people who were supposed to be pious and holy did not sit well with the Spanish faithful.

Radical New Ideas

But the demise of the Inquisition was perhaps most hastened by the French Revolution: the uprising, in 1789, of the common people of France against the aristocrats and the church. Both the nobility and the religious establishment were seen as keeping France from enjoying the benefits of democracy and justice. The ideas of individual liberty, religious and political tolerance, and equality were exciting new concepts for the French, and they wanted to destroy any institutions throughout Europe that stood in the way. The Spanish Inquisition, with its main offices then in Madrid, was one of the first on their list.

Led by Napoleon Bonaparte, French troops seized Madrid, and the victorious forces declared the oppressive Inquisition dead, although it survived in smaller tribunals around the country. It officially resur-

A Dispute over Fish

In his book The Spanish Inquisition, *Charles T. Gorham explains how popular opinion toward the Inquisition soured, especially because of the arrogance of the inquisitors. In this passage, he describes an incident at a fish market that resulted in a shamefully severe punishment for one man who dared to stand up against such arrogance.*

"[A]s long as the Holy Office confined itself to its recognized function of defending the faith and suppressing heresy it received the support of all classes of the population; but it evoked a general and bitter antagonism when it claimed superiority to the civil law, persistently encroached upon public and private rights, protected its of-

ficials in their misdemeanors, and invariably behaved with insufferable selfishness and arrogance. . . . Unending trouble and heated disputes were caused by the claim of the inquisitors and their underlings to special privileges in connection with conveyances and public markets. . . . The officers and slaves of the Holy Office . . . abused their authority to the utmost. One instance of this was particularly shameful. A gentleman at Cordova had bought a fish in the market, and refused to give it up to an acquaintance of a servant of an inquisitor. For this grave offense, he was punished with two hundred lashes and sent to the galleys."

Citizens celebrate the end of the Inquisition in Barcelona. After the Spanish Inquisition was quashed by Napoleon, it was resumed briefly, and finally ended in the early 1800s.

faced after Napoleon's defeat in 1813, but never regained its former strength. Some heretics were half-heartedly hunted down; the last person executed, in 1826, was a schoolmaster who reportedly had not accompanied his class to mass.

The obsession with *limpieza de sangre* lasted well into the twentieth century, even though such laws had long since been erased. Many Spaniards, however, continued to feel a need to keep family bloodlines and pedigrees "pure."

The hatred and violence that occurred for more than 350 years in Spain have been evaluated and studied by historians of all backgrounds. Some church historians look at the positive motives behind the Inquisition—even though they admit that the methods were terribly unfair. Others are dismayed by what they see as pure wickedness and cruelty.

Most historians agree, however, that a great many bad things were done in the name of a religion that professes love and forgiveness—and neither of these virtues was evident in the actions of the inquisitors. Tens of thousands of people were executed, and hundreds of thousands were harmed by the Spanish Inquisition. Many agree with Gorham that it "not merely retarded human progress for more than three centuries, but it brought a proud people to the brink of ruin." [102]

Notes

Introduction: The Flames and the Heat

1. Cecil Roth, *The Spanish Inquisition*. London: Robert Hale, 1937, pp. 106–107.
2. Henry Charles Lea, *A History of the Inquisition in Spain*, vol. 4. New York: Macmillan, 1907, p. 525.
3. Charles T. Gorham, *The Spanish Inquisition*. London: Watts, 1916, p. 1.

Chapter 1: The Making of an Institution

4. William Manchester, *A World Lit Only by Fire: The Medieval Mind and the Renaissance*. Boston: Little, Brown, 1992, pp. 11–12.
5. Manchester, *A World Lit Only by Fire*, p. 37.
6. Manchester, *A World Lit Only by Fire*, p. 130.
7. Fernand Hayward, *The Inquisition*. New York: Alba House, 1966, p. 31.
8. Hayward, *The Inquisition*, p. 24.
9. Hayward, *The Inquisition*, p. 31.
10. Quoted in G. G. Coulton, *Inquisition and Liberty*. New York: Macmillan, 1938, p. 99.
11. Quoted in Coulton, *Inquisition and Liberty*, p. 103.
12. Hoffman Nickerson, *The Inquisition: A Political and Military Study of Its Establishment*. London: John Bale, Sons, and Danielson, 1923, p. 192.
13. Quoted in E. Vacandard, *The Inquisition: A Critical and Historical Study of the Coercive Power of the Church*. Merrick, NY: Richwood Publishing, 1917. Reprint, 1977, p. 86.
14. Nickerson, *The Inquisition*, p. 195.
15. Jean Plaidy, *The Spanish Inquisition: Its Rise, Growth, and End*. New York: Citadel Press, 1967, p. 39.

Chapter 2: The Roots of Spain's Inquisition

16. Roth, *The Spanish Inquisition*, p. 20.
17. Roth, *The Spanish Inquisition*, pp. 18–19.
18. Roth, *The Spanish Inquisition*, p. 18.
19. Quoted in Jean Mariejol, *The Spain of Ferdinand and Isabella*. New Brunswick, NJ: Rutgers University Press, 1961, p. 226.
20. Mariejol, *The Spain of Ferdinand and Isabella*, p. 227.
21. Rafael Sabatini, *Torquemada and the Spanish Inquisition: A History*. London: Stanley Paul, 1937, pp. 76–77.
22. Thomas Hope, *Torquemada, Scourge of the Jews*. London: George Allen & Unwin, 1939, p. 43.
23. Cecil Roth, *A History of the Marranos*. New York: Schocken Books, 1932, p. 14.
24. Sabatini, *Torquemada and the Spanish Inquisition*, p. 62.
25. Quoted in Plaidy, *The Spanish Inquisition*, p. 105.
26. Plaidy, *The Spanish Inquisition*, p. 105.
27. Roth, *The Spanish Inquisition*, p. 21.
28. B. Netanyahu, *The Origins of the Inquisition in Fifteenth Century Spain*. New York: Random House, 1995, p. 157.
29. Quoted in Netanyahu, *The Origins of the Inquisition*, p. 159. Helpful section on the roots of the Inquisition.

30. Netanyahu, *The Origins of the Inquisition*, p. 159.
31. Gorham, *The Spanish Inquisition*, p. 5.
32. Henry Charles Lea, *The Moriscos of Spain: Their Conversion and Expulsion*. Westport, CT: Greenwood Press, 1968, p. 8.
33. Quoted in Henry Kamen, *The Spanish Inquisition*. London: Weidenfeld and Nicolson, 1965, p. 19.
34. Roth, *A History of the Marranos*, p. 17.
35. Roth, *A History of the Marranos*, p. 21.
36. Roth, *The Spanish Inquisition*, pp. 30–31.
37. Roth, *The Spanish Inquisition*, p. 21.
38. Roth, *The Spanish Inquisition*, p. 26.
39. Roth, *The Spanish Inquisition*, p. 26.
40. Plaidy, *The Spanish Inquisition*, p. 108.
41. Quoted in Plaidy, *The Spanish Inquisition*, p. 108.

Chapter 3: The Inquisition Comes to Spain

42. Quoted in Sabatini, *Torquemada and the Spanish Inquisition*, p. 55.
43. Hope, *Torquemada, Scourge of the Jews*, p. 33.
44. Quoted in Gorham, *The Spanish Inquisition*, p. 5.
45. Quoted in Hope, *Torquemada, Scourge of the Jews*, pp. 44–45.
46. Sabatini, *Torquemada and the Spanish Inquisition*, p. 74.
47. Quoted in Sabatini, *Torquemada and the Spanish Inquisition*, p. 80.
48. Quoted in Roth, *The Spanish Inquisition*, p. 43.
49. Quoted in Roth, *The Spanish Inquisition*, p. 43.
50. Quoted in Henry Kamen, *Inquisition and Society in Spain in the Sixteenth and Seventeenth Centuries*. Bloomington: Indiana University Press, 1985, p. 31.
51. Roth, *The Spanish Inquisition*, p. 47.
52. Plaidy, *The Spanish Inquisition*, p. 115.
53. Quoted in Kamen, *Inquisition and Society in Spain*, p. 34.
54. Roth, *The Spanish Inquisition*, p. 45.
55. Roth, *The Spanish Inquisition*, p. 47.
56. Maurice Rowdon, *The Spanish Terror: Spanish Imperialism in the Sixteenth Century*. New York: St. Martin's Press, 1974, p. 45.
57. Hope, *Torquemada, Scourge of the Jews*, p. 60.
58. Quoted in Hope, *Torquemada, Scourge of the Jews*, p. 63.
59. Hope, *Torquemada, Scourge of the Jews*, p. 63.
60. Quoted in Plaidy, *The Spanish Inquisition*, p. 121.
61. Quoted in Kamen, *The Spanish Inquisition*, p. 34.
62. Henry Charles Lea, *A History of the Inquisition of Spain*, vol. 1. New York: Macmillan, 1906, p. 233.
63. Quoted in Kamen, *Inquisition and Society in Spain*, p. 34.

Chapter 4: Eliminating Enemies

64. Plaidy, *The Spanish Inquisition*, p. 162.
65. Plaidy, *The Spanish Inquisition*, p. 162.
66. Sabatini, *Torquemada and the Spanish Inquisition*, p. 216.
67. Quoted in Sabatini, *Torquemada and the Spanish Inquisition*, p. 217.
68. Plaidy, *The Spanish Inquisition*, p. 163.
69. Quoted in Sabatini, *Torquemada and the Spanish Inquisition*, p. 218.
70. Sabatini, *Torquemada and the Spanish Inquisition*, p. 220.

71. Quoted in Hope, *Torquemada, Scourge of the Jews*, p. 193.
72. Quoted in Kamen, *Inquisition and Society in Spain*, p. 12.
73. Sabatini, *Torquemada and the Spanish Inquisition*, p. 283.
74. Hope, *Torquemada, Scourge of the Jews*, p. 195.
75. Quoted in Sabatini, *Torquemada and the Spanish Inquisition*, p. 277.
76. Plaidy, *The Spanish Inquisition*, pp. 172–73.
77. Quoted in Hope, *Torquemada, Scourge of the Jews*, p. 210.
78. Hope, *Torquemada, Scourge of the Jews*, p. 212.
79. Kamen, *Inquisition and Society*, p. 18.
80. Gorham, *The Spanish Inquisition*, pp. 75–76.
81. Quoted in Kamen, *Inquisition and Society*, p. 164.
82. Plaidy, *The Spanish Inquisition*, p. 128.

Chapter 5: Process and Punishment

83. Plaidy, *The Spanish Inquisition*, p. 129.
84. Plaidy, *The Spanish Inquisition*, p. 135.
85. Gorham, *The Spanish Inquisition*, p. 14.

86. Roth, *The Spanish Inquisition*, p. 94.
87. Roth, *The Spanish Inquisition*, p. 106.
88. Quoted in Roth, *The Spanish Inquisition*, p. 97.
89. Sabatini, *Torquemada and the Spanish Inquisition*, p. 191.
90. Quoted in Roth, *The Spanish Inquisition*, p. 98.
91. Quoted in Roth, *The Spanish Inquisition*, p. 98.
92. Plaidy, *The Spanish Inquisition*, p. 145.
93. A. S. Turberville, *The Spanish Inquisition*. London: Oxford University Press, 1932, p. 93.
94. Quoted in Roth, *The Spanish Inquisition*, p. 103.
95. Roth, *The Spanish Inquisition*, p. 104.
96. Quoted in Coulton, *Inquisition and Liberty*, p. 137.
97. Roth, *The Spanish Inquisition*, p. 121.
98. John A. O'Brien, *The Inquisition*. New York: Macmillan, 1973, p. 21.

Conclusion: A Gradual Demise

99. Gorham, *The Spanish Inquisition*, p. 87.
100. Gorham, *The Spanish Inquisition*, p. 89.
101. Gorham, *The Spanish Inquisition*, p. 90.
102. Gorham, *The Spanish Inquisition*, p. 119.

For Further Reading

Margaret Aston, *The Fifteenth Century: The Prospect of Europe*. New York: Harcourt, Brace, and World, 1968. Excellent illustrations, good section on travel in the fifteenth century.

Deborah Bachrach, *The Inquisition*. San Diego, CA: Lucent Books, 1995. Easy-to-read overview of both the early and Spanish Inquisitions.

Fernand Braudel, *The Structures of Everyday Life: Civilization and Capitalism, 15th–18th Century*, vol. 1. New York: Harper & Row, 1979. Excellent details on every aspect of European life during the reign of Ferdinand and Isabella. Helpful illustrations.

Barbara Brenner, *If You Were There in 1492*. New York: Bradbury Press, 1992. Easy reading, but good range of material on life in Spain at the time when the Inquisition was just beginning.

D. Juan Antonio Llorente, *The History of the Inquisition of Spain: From the Time of Its Establishment to the Reign of Ferdinand VII*. London: George B. Whittaker, 1827. Although sometimes difficult reading, the accounts of Llorente, who was an official of the Inquisition, are very important. Good section on witchcraft and the Inquisition.

Melveena McKindrick, *The Horizon Concise History of Spain*. New York: American Heritage, 1972. Good illustrations; helpful information about Isabella's background.

Works Consulted

G. G. Coulton, *Inquisition and Liberty*. New York: Macmillan, 1938. Excellent section on the beginnings of the original Inquisition in Europe.

Anne Fremantle, *The Age of Faith* (part of *Great Ages of Man Series*). New York: Time-Life Books, 1965. Very good material on corruption in the Catholic Church in pre-Inquisition Spain.

Charles T. Gorham, *The Spanish Inquisition*. London: Watts, 1916. Very small volume with lots of good information. Helpful section on the Spanish Inquisition's ban on books.

Fernand Hayward, *The Inquisition*. New York: Alba House, 1966. Helpful information about the Cathari and other heretical groups.

Geoffrey Hindley, *The Medieval Establishment*. New York: G. P. Putnam's Sons, 1970. Excellent illustrations, easy to understand.

Thomas Hope, *Torquemada, Scourge of the Jews*. London: George Allen & Unwin, 1939. Very readable account of Torquemada's life and influence on the Inquisition.

Henry Kamen, *Inquisition and Society in Spain in the Sixteenth and Seventeenth Centuries*. Bloomington: Indiana University Press, 1985. Very helpful introduction; good section on Isabella's dealings with Pope Sixtus.

———, *The Spanish Inquisition*. London: Weidenfeld and Nicolson, 1965. Glossary of important Spanish terms; good illustrations.

Henry Charles Lea, *A History of the Inquisition of Spain*, vols. 1 and 4. New York: Macmillan, 1906, 1907. Considered one of the most important of all works about the Spanish Inquisition. Excellent reference list.

———, *The Moriscos of Spain: Their Conversion and Expulsion*. Westport, CT: Greenwood Press, 1968. Helpful background information on the Moors and their influence in Spain.

William Manchester, *A World Lit Only by Fire: The Medieval Mind and the Renaissance*. Boston: Little, Brown, 1992. Invaluable material in a very readable style. Fascinating account of superstitions among the people of medieval Europe.

Deborah Manley, ed., *The Guinness Book of Records 1492*. New York: Facts on File, 1992. Excellent background reading about the world of 1492. Especially interesting section on medicine and disease.

Jean Hippolyte Mariejol, *The Spain of Ferdinand and Isabella*. Translated by Benjamin Keen. New Brunswick, NJ: Rutgers University Press, 1961. Helpful information on the social life of the Spanish people at the time of Columbus.

B. Netanyahu, *The Origins of the Inquisition in Fifteenth Century Spain*. New York: Random House, 1995. Extremely well researched; excellent endnotes and index.

Hoffman Nickerson, *The Inquisition: A Political and Military Study of Its Establishment*. London: John Bale, Sons, and

Danielson, 1923. Helpful section on the roots of the Inquisition.

John A. O'Brien, *The Inquisition*. New York: Macmillan, 1973. Interesting commentary on the Inquisition, since the author is very pro-church. Good bibliography.

Jean Plaidy, *The Spanish Inquisition: Its Rise, Growth, and End*. New York: Citadel Press, 1967. Very readable, especially good background on the monarchy in the regions of Spain before Ferdinand and Isabella.

Cecil Roth, *A History of the Marranos*. New York: Schocken Books, 1932. Often challenging reading, but well worth the effort for information about the life of the *marranos* in inquisitional Spain. Good index.

———, *The Spanish Inquisition*. London: Robert Hale, 1937. Very readable text, good section on torture and penances in the Inquisition of Spain.

Maurice Rowdon, *The Spanish Terror: Spanish Imperialism in the Sixteenth Century*. New York: St. Martin's Press, 1974. Good section on the defeat of Granada.

Rafael Sabatini, *Torquemada and the Spanish Inquisition: A History*. London: Stanley Paul, 1937. Very readable, helpful index.

A. S. Turberville, *The Spanish Inquisition*. London: Oxford University Press, 1932. Helpful information on the so-called *marranos*.

E. Vacandard, *The Inquisition: A Critical and Historical Study of the Coercive Power of the Church*. Merrick, NY: Richwood Publishing, 1917. Reprint, 1977. Good information on the involvement of various popes in the Inquisition.

Index

Queen Isabella and, 8, 40, 41

quemadero (burning place), 76–78

sanbenitos (garment), 75–76
Santo Niño, 75
Sixtus IV (pope), 40, 41
    orders Inquisition, 42–43
    protests Inquisition, 49–50
sorcery
    belief in, 25, 61
    crime of, 9, 59, 62
Spain
    anti-Semitism in, 26, 27, 33–35, 49, 55
    censorship of books in, 79–80, 81
    civil courts of, 46, 51, 76
    convivencia (amity) in, 26–27
    governs Inquisition, 9–10, 42, 50, 79
    Jews in, 26–39
        as *marranos*, 36–39
        success of, 27–28, 29–30, 55
    Moors and
        admiration for, 32
        reconquista and, 26, 27
        war with, 25, 27, 42, 79
    purity-of-blood laws in, 80–81
    standards of living in, 28–30
    Suprema in, 46, 51
Spanish Inquisition, 10, 11, 39, 81–83

accused persons in
    assumed guilty, 66–67
    Christians as, 9, 59
    conversos as, 43–45, 52
    dead people as, 9, 77
    heretics as, 22, 23–24
    humiliation of, 74–76
    marranos as, 43, 44, 48
    auto-da-fé in, 76–79
    courts of
        acquittal in, 9, 66
        interrogation in, 65–68
    dates of, 8, 12, 25, 74, 76, 83
    "familiars" in, 62–63, 65
    Holy Office of, 10, 50, 65, 82
    in Aragon, 51–54
    jails of, 8, 65, 66
    La Guardia case and, 56
    policies
        anonymity, 47
        bloodlines, 35, 80–81
        censorship of books, 9, 79–81
        confiscation of property, 11, 42, 51, 65, 82
        courts, 66–67, 76
        Edict of Faith, 60–62
        expulsion from country, 56–58, 74
        heretics, 22–24
        inquisitors, 43
        Instructions, 59–60
        papal bulls, 41, 42, 49–50
        relapsed Christians, 47–48
        torture, 70, 71–72

    purpose of, 10, 12, 20–21, 79
    records of, 8–11
    Seville and, 43, 46–50, 63
    tortures of, 8, 68–78
        burning, 11, 72, 75, 77–78
        execution, 10, 76–78
        hoists, 69–70
        potro, 70–71
        rack, 72
    voluntary confessions in, 63–64
    see also inquisitors
Spina, Alfonso de, 38–39
Suprema, 46, 51
Susan, Diego de, 45–46

Talavera, Hernando de, 32
Torquemada, Alvar
    Fernandez, 47
Torquemada, Tomás, 40–41, 42, 47
    Edict of Faith and, 60–62
    grants anonymity to accusers, 46–47, 49
    in Castile, 43
    Instructions and, 59–60
    plans expansion, 51–52
    relapsed Christians and, 47–48, 54
    sanbenitos revived by, 75–76
    targets Jews, 54–57
    tortures accused, 68–69

witchcraft
    belief in, 25, 61
    crime of, 9, 59, 62

Picture Credits

Cover photo: AKG, London
Archive Photos, 24, 66
Bridgeman/Art Resource, NY, 36
Corbis-Bettmann, 20, 21, 28, 45, 48, 51, 58, 60, 64, 70, 71, 81
Giraudon/Art Resource, NY, 16, 26, 83

Erich Lessing/Art Resource, NY, 41, 42
Library of Congress, 22, 31, 43, 80
North Wind Picture Archives, 13, 18
Popperfoto, 55
Stock Montage, Inc., 34, 56, 62, 67

About the Author

Gail B. Stewart received her undergraduate degree from Gustavus Adolphus College in St. Peter, Minnesota. She did her graduate work in English, linguistics, and curriculum study at the College of St. Thomas and the University of Minnesota. She taught English and reading for more than ten years.

She has written over ninety books for young people, including a series for Lucent Books called The Other America. She has written many books on historical topics such as World War I and the Warsaw Ghetto.

Stewart and her husband live in Minneapolis with their three sons, Ted, Elliot, and Flynn, two dogs, and a cat. When she is not writing she enjoys reading, walking, and watching her sons play soccer.